INVISIBLE PAIN

Letters to My Dad

INVISIBLE PAIN

Letters to My Dad

Anthony Outen

BOATWATER BOOKS
RICHMOND VIRGINIA

First Edition, Printed in the United States of America

Published by:
Boatwater Books
PO Box 935
Richmond, Virginia 23218

ISBN: 0615598811
ISBN-13: 978-0-615-59881-9

*This is an epistolary work, included are many real life situations from the author's memory. To preserve the anonymity of those people who may not feel I portrayed them in a good light, I have changed their names to protect them. Many of the names are the actual persons from my life and memories, and I wish to thank them.

To my grandparents Elizabeth and Rufus Outen
Thanks for making me your son.

TABLE OF CONTENTS

TRUTH AND CONSEQUENCES

IN EACH OF OUR LIVES, EVERYDAY offers new challenges and new possibilities. For some, the days feel overwhelming and empty because of the pain carried from an identity crisis that is not of our own making. In recent generations, many men have been absent from the duties of fatherhood for various reasons. There are many excuses; however, in my opinion, there are none that hold true validity. The creation of life requires sacrifice, honesty, and a passion to influence the life created.

There are three categories of children with visible and *invisible pain*: 1) those that have never met or known who their father is, 2) those that know their father but he has never made any contribution to their life, and 3) the father who is at home but has other things to do than love and nurture their child. My story falls under the first category never meeting or having any knowledge of who my father is or where I came from. Regardless of which category best relates to you or the person you know, you may agree that each causes pain, anger, and often leads to circumstances that result in emotional trauma and complex personalities.

When you yearn for an identity and validation of your father and you have never received it, you will find yourself in a *"make believe"* world of illusions of who you are not. This was the case for me for so many years. As you read the pages to follow, you will see that life had no boundaries. A person's life is not defined by where they are born, how rich their family may be, or how poor they may be for that matter. People are people. We all share the same characteristics that make us more alike than different.

Everyone suffers, everyone hurts, and yes, everyone at some time or another regardless of their circumstances do smile from time to time. I, like many who will read these letters, have experienced all of these emotions, and I have handled each of them differently. There you will find *Invisible Pain*. We are all here, not by anyone or anything we see, but because of what we don't see but know exist within us.

Like many, I have walked around on occasion searching for things that have always been there. This story is a healing process. Until recently, I had no clue I needed healing. The emotions are raw, some funny, some interesting, some painful, but they are a reflection of the challenges and the miracles that allow me to sit and write with the hope that someone will see himself or recognize someone she knows and can find peace for things in life over which we have no control.

Pain for the most part is *invisible*. Sure, there are signs of trauma that reflect obvious pain, but the daily struggles that one carries within aren't seen but felt through emotions that often shatter the heart and weaken the mind not enabling us to experience the victory at the end of the struggle. Some attempt to cover pain with money, expensive gifts, and other possessions that can never substitute for truth, honesty, and real love. Time does not heal all wounds. The only way to deal with *invisible pain* is to see it for what it is a manipulative feeling which prevents the mind from seeing the possibilities of good in the midst of struggle.

Perhaps my reason for the writing these letters is to bring healing for something I always wanted as a child but never received. I'm not saying that I was not loved or that I was abused or lacking for anything essential. I was "spoiled" to the extent you could be in those days and our family's situation. I am a believer in finding the turning points in your life. Because there have been so many people that have shaped my life for the good and for the bad, I have become a very complex individual. Those who got to know me had no clue about who I really was inside, and in some respects, I had come to the point of asking that very question of myself. Though not intentionally, I managed to isolate myself from the very people who have meant the most to me.

These letters began as a result of a late night episode of Oprah's Master Class. She made a statement that spoke directly to me. Paraphrasing her words: *In order to truly be a success and happy within yourself, you must be yourself.*

You can never succeed by wanting to or trying to live your life through someone else or like someone else. As I continued to watch the show, I asked myself the simple question: *Who am I?* I couldn't answer that question. I hadn't thought about who I was or that not knowing who I was had been my problem. Since I did not understand my own identity, I couldn't be satisfied, so as a result, I was never a confident. I had no idea of where and when I lost myself or why for that matter. On the surface, it appeared to those around me that I was fully aware of who I was and what I wanted. I began to ask myself a series of questions and realized I needed to crack the code of what defines me or face a life of loneliness and emptiness.

In the 1970s, *The Waltons* was a popular television program depicting life focused on strong family values and loyalties. For a long time, I desired to document my life and the struggles of my family just like John Boy did. Although the show does not depict anyone who looks like me, it did speak to me of the sacred loyalties of a family and a respect that one can only dream of and wish for. The support of a father bonding with his son fascinated me. From the grandfather through the father to the son, this father/son relationship was something I greatly admired. The embracing of generational history and family values builds character and fulfills the legacy of support and love for things far more valuable than the superficial, material things of this world.

So, in my own words, let the healing begin as I share with you the *Invisible Pain* that began with a simple question: *Who am I?* and has turned into a journey of personal reflection and healing of my mind and soul.

DEAR DAD,

HOW YOU CAME TO KNOW MY mother and the relationship the two of you shared is a mystery to me. Although I have never seen your face, heard your voice, or have any true sense of the man you are, I feel it is imperative to write you. My desire is to write you a letter, one that will hopefully help me find who I am, and where I lost myself wanting so much to know you. My mother never spoke of you, and to many in our family, you have been sheltered in secrecy as if to protect a dark family secret. There have been times when I searched for you with the little information I had, but all along I've felt uncertain if any of the information was true. There have been so many lies told, so many inconsistencies in so many different stories. I find it difficult to believe that anyone is telling the truth, but I am closing that chapter of ceaseless questioning and doubts today with this letter to you.

I am a grown man now and have been blessed with three children of my own, two boys and one girl. I have done for them what you have not done for me. This is closure for me and for my children a legacy of truth about what I know of my life. I hold no anger or hatred towards you. I have finally come to terms with your non-existence in my life. I have managed to survive the complex circumstances I faced in my early years without you, and still I'm blessed. I was forced to live with many insecurities, many dramatic life-changing situations, but somehow I survived without a father's guidance that would have been so helpful. There is something about you that has made me who I am, and for that I say - *Thank you*. As far as I'm concerned my life began as a lie. If not by your doing totally, still as a man a great deal of responsibility for that rests with you. This is how I feel, and in this healing process, I'm just being honest and straight about it.

Since we do not know each other, I find it important to share these words with you about the life I've lived. Perhaps you can see through my eyes the pain you inflicted on me when you failed in your responsibilities. There have been life-changing, life-twisting circumstances that were possibly avoidable and many people who have tried to fill in for you. However, in my opinion and experience, there can never be a substitute for a real father's love and support. Because of you, I have dedicated my life to ensure that history will not repeat itself with another generation of the seed of your grandchildren being fatherless. For years, I sacrificed my own happiness to ensure theirs, and I've learned through it all any father is better than no father at all. The pain of you not being there to guide me when I was at the turning point of my teenage years could have been avoided if only you cared enough to be there and show me how to be a man and share your wisdom that to this day you never have. I suffered from depression and not being able to be who I really am and coming to grips with where I came from during parts of my life because of you, but still I survived. I could have been a drug addict as a young man, but God placed many positive men and women in my life to give me direction and instill hope like Mr. Lester, Ms. Williams, and Mrs. Boltz. I became a teenage father (Were you?) and for years had to learn how to relate and show love to my son, because I never learned those things from you. I didn't understand my role because you never fulfilled yours. So because of you, Dad, I failed for a while but survived in victory to say I didn't become you but learned to be a better me.

I remember watching my favorite show the *Waltons*. It said to me that this is the role of a father. I watched how the grandfather related to the father who related to John Boy. Here's a grandfather that has taught his son to be a dad, and the grandfather now has the opportunity to watch his son become a father. The grandfather was able to still give wisdom to his grandson through the father. Even though I never experienced this kind of relationship myself, it showed a realness of what I wanted to give to my children. It also showed how you were absent. I couldn't understand how a TV show could do this, and you couldn't. Your absence made me sit in front of a TV show and learn how to be a father instead of you being there as my father and teaching me yourself.

Ironically, late one night, I was watching some reruns of *The Waltons* and becoming depressed as I sat there in my bed. I started channel-surfing and ran across *Oprah's Master Class*. She talked about doubting herself, she realized she couldn't be Barbara Walters or anyone else for that matter, and didn't know how to pretend to be Barbara Walters. She said she just had to be "the best Oprah" not pattern her life after someone else. I listened to that. She said; as long as you pretend to be somebody else, you can never be the best you can be. She looked into the camera, and it was as if she was speaking only to me, and asked "Who are you?" She was defining who she was, but it was a defining moment for helping me define my inner feelings. She said you have to be the best "you". I realized that it wasn't me she was speaking, but her words were speaking to my soul. I had to figure out who I was at that moment to be a success tomorrow. In that moment I didn't know who I was. You weren't there, Dad. She asked the question several times, and I couldn't answer the question. I didn't know where I lost myself. I had no clue who I was so how could I be "the best me"? I didn't know who my father was. I felt I had to pretend to be somebody else for people to like me or appreciate me. So I lived this life of lies to trying to create the perfect image from TV characters and from everything else. It's like I was saying "This is what a family is" and "I need to be this person, like Victor Newman, because this character is powerful". So I created my father into this "powerful" guy for others.

I have to figure out who I am. So, after that show, I got paper and pencil and began to write you a letter to share with you why I feel the way I do and share, my life, my trials, my struggles, and my tribulations. Maybe by writing this letter, I can figure out who I am, when I lost myself, and why I feel the way I do. I had to start from my beginning. So I remembered the houses, what my grandmother told me, and looked back at my life with these words to you, and so I could begin to find myself.

For me, writing has always been my passion and the very thing that kept me from losing everything. Most of my stories about you and my childhood were told to me by my grandmother and various family members. These stories are coming back to me, some like a dreamy fog, some like a waterfall, as I piece together the history of my life. I want my children to understand and know where they came from and why they don't understand many of their father's behaviors. I want them to be able to look back with their children and understand who they are and to never lose themselves through the years by not being thankful for whom they are and the blessings they have. I can now say that I have taken things for granted and the things for which I searched were just packaged in a different way that wasn't ideal for what I defined as success.

It is important to say that when a man never meets his father, never learns who is his father, and from where he came, it is virtually impossible for him to be his *real self*. A man needs and will forever yearn to know his past, so that he can appreciate the possibilities of his future – not someone else's but his own. When my friends would talk about their fathers, I would make up stories about you. I would pretend to have things I didn't have, so that I could fit in with their world and not be on the outside looking in. I created a world of make-believe and after a period of time I came to believe the fabrications myself, as my reality, as my history. Because of these illusions and reckless behavior, there have been so many consequences.

What began as simple act of wanting to seem like everyone else eventually became a pattern of lies and deceit. There is only one end to the truth, but a lie has no ending as one lie always leads to another. You can never live up to your full potential if the "potential" is based on make-believe dreams of who you want to be rather than the reality of who you are. The fact I have the need to write to you today is a testament to your absence. The fact that I can write to you today is a testament to the many people that became the role models that you weren't for me.

Respectfully,

Anthony

DAD, THIS IS WHAT I UNDERSTAND TO BE MY BEGINNING.

MY BIRTHPLACE WAS ON A FARM called Harmon Hill; however, my earliest memories of life are from living on McLeod's Peach Farm, just off Highway 1 outside of McBee, South Carolina. My grandparents, Elizabeth and Rufus Outen, had always worked on farms, harvesting by hand everything from cotton to peaches. For working the farm, the owners granted them shelter in one of the ragged farm houses scattered around the properties. There was never any running water or indoor plumbing, but it was shelter and a place to call home. You could hardly complain, because in those days, you were just thankful to have a place to stay and for the family to be together. That's what my grandmother would often say.

Granddad, while sober, was a man of few words on any subject. It was the taste of alcohol that turned him into a very different person. I never understood why he was so angry and bitter when he would drink, but you can only imagine the torture he endured at the hands of those for whom he worked, because at any moment, a worker could lose his job and the house in which he lived, much less the degrading way he was treated. I believe the way Granddad escaped the wrath of cruel treatment was by drinking. A Drink allowed him the courage to say what he could not, or would not, while he was sober.

Granddad would work hard in the fields Monday through Friday, but Friday evenings through Sunday mornings would prove to be a living nightmare for the entire family. His relentless outbursts would unfold from the countless bottles of alcohol he would consume. At times, his behavior was very embarrassing since we lived next door to the church and in such a small town. Granddad was also a proud man, but now looking back, I think that the treatment he received working in the fields during all those years had a tremendous impact on his life.

Grandma never drank, and if she had, I think it would be fair to say that she and her children may not have made it through those tough days. She was a force to be reckoned with and will always be the best in my eyes. She was well-respected in the community, and she always walked with her head high and with tremendous pride regardless of her circumstances. My grandparents struggled financially their entire lives, but never can I recall a time they didn't pull though the struggle with pride. I don't recall my grandmother complaining a lot, but I remember her constantly praying. She never blamed anyone for her situation and wasn't one to care about people that made excuses. I never knew how bad things were or how poor we were, because there were so many others in the same situation around us. We were poor by every measure, but Grandmas' pride, grace, and dignity camouflaged it from my sight.

Grandma told me many stories about her life - some good, some hurtful, and sad. She told me about the story of my life, about how I was born, about her struggles in life, and about a wonderful wealth of history on that side of the family, but I have no knowledge of you, because you weren't there. I don't know my grand-parents on your half of my family. Do I walk or talk or have mannerisms that come from your side? Perhaps this letter will give you the opportunity to know your son, but you offered no love, no support, no guidance, and no opportunity to know your family and its history by nonexistence.

I want to share with you a little about my great-grandparents, and some of the experiences I had with my grandmother and some of my family. It is rare that you have the opportunity to know and live with your great-grandmother. I'm thankful to say that I had that opportunity since my great-grandfather, Moody, died before I was born. Great-grandma Morgan was a woman of strength and courage, and unlike many in those days, she was a woman of financial stability. She lived in a home not owned by the white farmer or businessman. My great-grandparents were blessed to be among the few African-American families to have a deeded property, a rarity in the early 1900s. Most black people only owned the clothes on their backs and a few furnishings for the home. My great-grandparents' life began in Lee County, South Carolina. This is where my grandmother, Elizabeth, was born, who raised me. They would later relocate their family to Hartsville, South Carolina, and build a home there. It was also quite rare in those days to have indoor plumbing and running water, but they did. Not to mention, the home was inside the city limits and not off in the back-woods or on a dirt road, another rarity for black families in those days. I'm not certain that the home always had these luxuries – and to me they were luxuries indeed - but they were present as far back as I can remember as a child. I remember well that Great-grandma had a telephone, because my grandmother would make her calls on it for business or to confer with family she didn't get to speak to during the week. Most of Great-grandma's children lived up north, but when her local brothers, Uncle Jessie and Uncle Major, knew she was in town, you could rest assured that they would show up for hours of stories and good laughs. The property is still in the family, but the house is gone. I recall the family home was simple by design. The house was white with black shutters and had a full front porch. I still remember many Saturday afternoon gatherings of our family on that front porch. The backyard was small, so most activities would take place in the driveway on the right side where there were large shade trees. The big shade tree at the entrance of the driveway where my brothers and sisters and I sat and played when we would visit still stands amidst the ruins of the family home - a sentinel to the generations.

On the corner of the street on the left side of my great-grandmother's house was a little corner store owned by an old woman. The store was in front, and she lived in the back portion of the building. I loved to go over there and buy cookies, candy, and the occasional ice cream cone. I can still remember the big cookie jars on the counters and the excitement of reach-ing into jars to get as many cookies that my few pennies could buy. I would be in pure heaven if I could trade enough empty bottles to buy a cold drink from the icebox. Those are truly remarkable memories that I cherish and how it would have meant so much if some of those walks to the store could have been shared with you. I have often thought what it would have been like to walk with you back then when I walk my own children today to the store or to anything of significance. What would it have been like to have you be with me back then? I even think about something as simple as taking my son to the barber shop and waiting for him. What would it have been like if you sat and waited for me at the barber shop? No one really sat there with me. Even at times when I sit in the stands and watch my son run plays in football, after all these years, I still have thoughts of what it would have meant to me if you could have sat and watched me in band while in school.

As the many years of age and long life began to run its course on the health of my great-grandmother, Eliza, it became clear that she would not be able to stay in her home alone. At first, she spent some time with her daughter, Freda, who is my great aunt and my grandmother's sister in Georgia, but she became somewhat homesick and wanted to be closer to her house in Hartsville, South Carolina. Aunt Freda had taken care of her for some time, but in her declining health Great-grandmother wanted to come live with my grandmother. My grandmother was very close to her sister, Freda, and I can never recall a time when they didn't work so well together taking care of Great-grandma. Aunt Freda always smiled and was so cheerful and often went out of her way to make everyone feel positive and loved. She made sure that everything stayed in place and in proper order at Great-grandmas' house for the entire time she lived with us. We always looked forward to her visits, and there were so many. She often would check on her mother and offer what support she could to my grandmother.

With Great-grandma's arrival also came many additional visits from my grandmother's brothers and sisters than would have typically happened. It was almost like having a family reunion week after week. Having Great-grandma live with us was new territory, but everyone adjusted to it very well. A very soft-spoken woman, she liked what she liked, and she had many old fashioned home remedies. I can remember how she would have me to collect the hardened sap from pine trees. When pine tar dried, it turned a dark brown and became very crunchy. I collected it in clean jars and brought it all to her. It was such a cool task to do. She said it was good for arthritis. I'm not sure it worked, but it was rare that she complained about aching.

Great-grandma would sit in the yard under the large oak trees with my grandmother, and they would talk and laugh for hours. There were also times when she would sit in the shade and just hum songs as she glanced around exploring her surroundings. You could only imagine the thoughts she must have been having. She appeared to be so at peace, and I imagine that some of her thoughts were joyous in nature. Perhaps she realized her decision to give my grandmother the money to buy the land for the house where she would spend her final days was a good decision. Wisdom has its place and you should always seek to be wise in your daily life. Great-grandma could never get my name right. Instead of Anthony, she always said Ankum. It didn't matter; I knew what she was saying, and besides, you did not correct your elders in those days if you liked your teeth. When you were called by whatever name, you answered.

For Great-grandma to get around, Aunt Lula Mae, who lived in Hartsville, would drive her and my grandmother around. She would come and visit often. Because she had a car, she would bring Great-grandma's medication refills. As for Great-grandma, she sure enjoyed spending time with her daughters. On some days for therapy, my grandmother and her sister would put Great-grandma in the car and take her for a ride to Hartsville so she could see her old house. They would let her go through the rooms to make sure things were just as she left them. She seemed satisfied with that, and as I think back, it was wonderful to show her that love and respect. So many times, elderly family members don't get the respect they deserve. My entire life was molded by women who had already raised their children and who still took the time to share love, affection and caring for the well-being of others.

There were other times that my great-grandma's youngest son, Frank, would come from New York with his lovely wife, Aunt Carrie, and my cousins, Rome and Lena. Like my Uncle Jamie, Uncle Frank is also an ordained minister and pastor. I looked forward to those visits perhaps more than any other family visits. I always enjoyed the great times I would have with my cousins. Uncle Frank was always full of laughs; he was like the junior comedian of the family with his brother, Major the senior. He always had snappy comebacks and often tried to be the intimidator, but I soon learned that his bark was louder than the little bite you ended up with. He would pull into the driveway with his super long Cadillac's and tricked-out conversion vans. When I was about 11, I thought he was the richest person in the world. Very few Cadillac's pulled into our yard, and I was always filled with amazement. I guess you could say I have always had a love and a fascination with fine automobiles. I felt so cool when he would give me a ride, and I was extremely excited whenever he let me sit in the front seat. He and my grandmother would often lock horns, but she still loved him dearly. Besides that, she always won! When it was dinnertime, we would all gather around the dinner table and eat until someone wanted to take a nap. My cousins and I would go outside and have the greatest laughs. We wanted those visits to last forever. Do I get my fascination of fine automobiles and flashy cars from you, Dad?

There would also be visits from Uncle Raymond. Uncle Raymond lived in New York, and he was the mildest-mannered of my great-grand-mother's sons. He didn't care for flashy Cadillac's, but instead he had a big blue Plymouth that looked like it was a mile long. This is the only car I remember him driving and the first car I had ever seen with an alarm system. He would stick his key in the front fender to activate it, and I eagerly awaited the loud sound of the horns. I'd even run and get the neighborhood kids so they could hear the alarm. This was long before remote activators, and it was very rare for someone to have a car alarm. I remember his nice car stereo and maybe that was the reason for the alarm. He loved to listen to James Brown on his 8-track player. I remember sitting under the tree with my uncles while the music was playing in his car as they admired the sound. It seems funny writing about an 8-track stereo sound system being protected by an alarm system today.

Now, Uncle Major was in a league all by himself. He lived in Hartsville and loved his big Cadillac's like his younger brother, Frank. Most would agree he was the most eccentric of all of his brothers and sisters. Great-grandma would have to calm him down, because he was always extremely loud. His hearing wasn't that great, but my grandmother always said that he heard what he really wanted to hear. If he asked you to repeat yourself, it only meant that he wasn't interested in what you had to say. He loved his garden just as my grandmother loved hers. He would often bring her fresh vegetables and take some things from hers back home with him. There was never any question who made my grandmother laugh the most. That would certainly be Uncle Major.

There was also a serious side to him, and everyone knew it. Never cross Uncle Major, or there would certainly be major consequences. Most people say, "Hello, how are you today?" when they greet you but not him.

His greeting was to everyone - no matter who you were or what you were - "Let me see your wacker!" It was always hilarious. Wish you'd been there, Dad, to see him in action. Aunt Jennie always had her hands full with her wild husband. Aunt Jennie was a kind gentle woman who endured then and continues to smile and shake her head at the crazy things he continues to say and do.

Aunt Pearlene, another of my great-grandmother's daughters, was considered the family matriarch. She was much older, and everyone looked up to her and would seek her guidance on many issues concerning Great-grandma and other family matters. She never raised her voice, and she always loved to do Great-grandma's hair. Aunt Pearlene lived in New York, and my mother lived with her during her stay there. Maybe you met her when you dated my mom before I was born. If you did, I'm sure you discovered the wonderful spirit of humility within her.

Even though Great-grandma was surrounded by the love of many children, grandchildren, and great-grandchildren, that could not sustain her health. Eventually, we were faced with the sadness of great-grandma being too ill to live with us. My grandmother had done all she could do, but the hospital was more equipped to give her the care she needed. For a very short time, she had to go to a nursing home, but God didn't let her linger and suffer very long. In September of 1978, she went home to be with the Lord.

Dad, the reason I want to share this information about my family with you is I really want to give you a snapshot into my life as a young kid and the many moments of love and pain from those that guided me. Although I haven't told you about my grandmother's brothers, Uncle Jessie and Uncle Hazel, you haven't told me about you or my uncles and aunts on your side of my family. There's a void in my identity and family history that I deserved to know, and you as my father should have wanted to share with me as I have shared with you. I think I know maybe something about your sister, Tina, and I often wondered how many fun reunions I could have been a part of on your side of my family tree. I thought about that a lot as a kid. There have been times I walked around New York and New Jersey and saw people on the streets. Could any of these people have been a part of my family? When I was younger, I often sat in restaurants and looked across the room and noticed people that would stare at me, and I wondered if they think they know me, because I looked like you. Were they a part of my family? Did they see something in me that was a part of something in you? Every time I see someone who seems to recognize me, I wonder. People have said to me, "You look like someone I know," and I sometimes reply, "Well, could be. My father is somewhere in New York, and I've never met him, so maybe so." Or when I sat in restaurants and looked at families interacting with each other, I thought why can't I have that? Your absence was always present.

Anthony

DAD, I OFTEN WONDERED WAS I A MIRACLE OR MISTAKE?

SOMETIME IN 1963, THE YOUNGEST OF my grandparent's children, my aunt Mildred, entered school. This meant that my grandmother would be home alone during the day, and she began to slip into what she described in later years as a time of major depression and loneliness. During this time, my grandfather was exerting a physical and emotional pattern of extremely abusive behavior. There was nothing or anyone to break the agony of her days. There was no one to show her love, so she prayed for anything that might lessen the anger and cruelty of my grandfather's relentless rage.

Sadly through the day, she would sit at home and weep. She began to play and talk to life-size dolls as if they were real. She said that she felt so alone, unwanted, unloved at times and simply didn't know what to do. Even though there were still children in the home, something had changed. She would explain and go into detail the abuse and torture she was going through and what she had been experiencing for years. It demonstrated the penetrating agony of her lonely heart, and this stands out so clearly in my memory to this very day.

A woman of strong faith, she came to the conclusion that the only thing she could do was to pray. Always having a very close relationship with God with strong spiritual convictions, she believed in the power of prayer. When all else failed, she could always find the healing comforts of God in her secret closet. Accepting that at her age there would be no more children, she still desired of the Lord that he would grant her some company during the day.

She needed someone or something to help heal her mind. *This was her constant prayer she would tell me later.* She would receive this little spiritual magazine, *Life Study Fellowship,* which still comes to many of her children and grandchildren's homes today. This was her inspirational reading along with her *Bible* verses. In this magazine are testimonies, daily prayers, and poems of inspiration. There were three prayers you were to read every day. One for morning, afternoon, and evening that I can never remember her failing to take the time for each day. No matter where she would travel, in her purse was this magazine to read and meditate on the things she desired of God. She always planned her life around these prayers for as long as I can remember.

There is one particular story that always gained traction at most family gatherings. They thought it strange, as did she, to constantly ask God for another child when it was obvious that she could not have any more children, yet she refused to lose hope and continued to pray. She always had faith that God was going to answer her prayer for another child in the house. When my mother, Doretha, after working in the peach fields in the summer with her brothers and sisters like so many others, wanted to escape the farm life of the Deep South, she made the decision to quit school even though she had met a man while working there, and things were somewhat alright. She wanted to move to New York and live with my grandmother's sisters and brothers around the vicinity of Roosevelt and Long Island, New York, and search for work. She wanted to see something new, something not a peach farm, to experience a different way of life. My mother was quite adventurous and ahead of her time in many respects. A very smart woman, she realized that her life's potential could not be achieved working in the peach fields of South Carolina. She simply wanted more than that and felt there was so much more she wanted to see and a life in New York would give that to her.

During those days, it was not unusual for there to be advertisements for jobs up north in southern newspapers and magazines. It was in one of these publications that my mother answered an ad to become a nanny. Through some process and planning, the New York family sent a small travel allowance and a ticket for Mom to go to New York. This would be her break and the prelude to her meeting you.

Eventually, after the advertised position had been confirmed legitimate and arrangements were satisfactory to my grandmother, Grandmother gave her blessings and allowed my mother to go. Eager to explore and to create the best life she could for herself, my mom left home for the big city. This was a major step for my mom and also for my grandmother to watch her first-born daughter leave home at such a young age with nothing more than a dream and a prayer. She would stay with her Aunt Pearlene, my grandmother's sister, until she was settled in with her new job. As time went on, Mom would eventually find solitude working as a nanny for a somewhat wealthy family in upstate New York. Soon she moved in with the family and helped raise the two young daughters of the upstate family. Excited to be there, she often worked on her days off, taking the girls to the park and to the movies. The family paid her well, gave her room and board, and actually treated her as one of their family. She began to come into her own, venture out, and make friends as she explored the fast-paced life of the city. She even began to send money home as was customary in those days to help the family. According to my grandmother, she appeared happy with her life. She was content with her job and adjusting well to living in the city.

At some point, my mother met you. On the rare occasions, my aunts would say she fell madly in love with you. But I would speculate differently. Something between you and my mother had to have been awful at the end. The way I'm imagining it is that my mom was a young, inexperienced county girl from South Carolina and went to the big city, New York. She met a man who has street smarts and savvy. She was introduced to things she had never imagined. You took advantage of her inexperience. I believe she expected you to be more than you turned out to be. So, whatever you did to hurt her was such a devastating blow, it was unforgiveable and was something that got her to a point she didn't return to you or talk about you or forgave you. Of all the people that my mom would take issue with or had problems with, she still talked about them, but when it came to you, I have very little information about you, except that which was given to me by various family members. She didn't even share the good memories much less the bad ones. It must have been something very significant for her never to want to talk about you, something in the relationship that was too painful for her to speak of. She didn't want to deal with it, and she wasn't a weak person. Whatever you did put her at a turning point that she didn't want to deal with that pain. This letter is me dealing with my *invisible pain*. Most of what I was told about you I have discovered is mostly lies. However, my grandmother would always say, "*To every lie, there is some truth.*"

On many occasions, I was told your name is Sam; however, some have said your name is Anthony, and I was named partly after you. Which is true? Because really, Dad, I have no idea. I was also told your last name is Thomas. Another mystery so I'm left to wonder what is real and what is fabrication. Perhaps no one knows, Dad, and everyone wants to be a hero by pretending to know something that they don't. I was told that your mother was a nurse and that my grandfather worked for the New York Police Department. They said your brothers owned various convenience stores around the city, and you had some interest in music. It came to be my understanding that you were the leader of a popular band and often played concerts. Again, I have no real idea about what is true or false. I have no facts to back these ideas up. My mother was quite fond of your sister, Tina, apparently how she met you in the first place, but that is it. That's the only thing I really know to this day.

No one knows exactly how long my mother was in a relationship with you before she became pregnant or how long the relationship lasted after it was discovered that she was pregnant. However, after I was born, my mother went back to you in New York for a few months, but then whatever awful things happened drove her back to the farm in South Carolina. Back then, as you know, it was not at all "proper" and was heavily frowned upon for any girl or woman to become pregnant and not married. However, these were not normal circumstances. My mother was trying to figure out what to do, pregnant and unmarried, couldn't stay in New York and be a nanny to other children. What were her options? At one point, she even considered having an abortion or putting me up for adoption; thereby, avoiding to tell my grandmother anything. She was just so afraid of bringing shame to my grandmother and afraid of the strict hand and wrath of Elizabeth if Grandmother's rules and expectations were broken. I have put together fragments of this from small exchanges with my aunts.

Sometime in September of 1965, it became evident to my mother that she was not going to be able to keep her pregnancy a secret. Being a live-in nanny with child was not going to work either. She knew that if she went to her aunts' and uncles' surely they were going to tell my grandmother. So there she was stuck in a big city with little or no emotional support and with her options getting slimmer and slimmer. I'm not sure what happened, if she got the courage from within, if you encouraged her, or if it came from the words of some of her friends, but one day she finally decided to make that dreaded telephone call *Home*.

Somehow, Mom and Grandma managed to speak by telephone, and as the conversation continued, a frightened young woman uttered the words that would from that point on change her life and my grandmother's forever. I imagine the conversation went something like this: "Momma, I have something bad to tell you." "What is it, Doretha?" "I'm pregnant." I can only imagine, given those times and circumstances, the utter agony my mother must have been feeling. Then she heard the words she was not expecting nor ever thought she would hear from my grandmother. "That's fine. You come on home now. The Lord will make a way, and I've been praying for a child to keep me company, and my prayers have been answered. Bring that blessing home. I'm not angry; everything is fine. There is nothing for you to be afraid of. This is God's doing."

By the time my mother would arrive back in McBee, she would be seven months pregnant with me. Everyone rallied together, her sisters, and brothers along with my grandparents to care for my mother. It wasn't a time of neither shame nor anger in any sense of the word. My grandfather was always quite fond of my mother, probably his favorite; to him, she could do no wrong. Although he rarely was the disciplinarian (those decisions were left to my grandmother), he was supportive. I do know that of all my grandfathers' children my mother felt the closest to him, and that bond was never broken. She never seemed to be disturbed by his drinking and outbursts. She always respected him as her father. In many ways, she was the only one to not hold any resentment towards him for his abusive behavior towards Grandma. She allowed no one to disrespect him regardless of his actions.

According to my grandmother, I was born during one of the coldest winters she had ever experienced. Late into the cold winter night of December 1, 1965, my mother began to go into labor. As the sun began to rise on the morning of December 2, 1965, and after caring for my mother, Grandma realized she had done all she could do, and it was time to prepare for the birth of her first grandchild. She told my grandfather to go to the home of the town midwife, Ms. Emma Tillman. Ms. Tillman was known to have delivered many of the black children around McBee in those days including many of my grandmothers' children. If you did not have the money for hospitals or any form of insurance which was the case with us and for many others, Ms. Tillman was your saving grace.

In those days, there were few interior doors. You would hang sheets over the doorways for privacy. This made it very easy for sounds to be heard throughout the house as well as an occasional glimpse at the activities in the other room. There was constant running back and forth to the stove for fresh hot water and cleaning of soiled towels from the childbirth activities. It's amazing how without any medication women back then gave birth in conditions like that.

When it was all said and done, I was born on that 2nd day of December thus marking the beginning of life for me and big changes for the entire family. Mom, free of her fear of telling her parents she was with child, realized life was not over and still had hope. My grandmother felt her prayers had been answered, and there was never any mention of her feeling depressed or playing with life-size dolls after my birth. Grandma was thankful and dedicated her life to raising me. Although these events are from my grandmother's perspective only, I am not sure if my mother felt the same way. Perhaps she did not and felt it would be best to leave things as they were after I was born, leave me in my grandmother's care while she went back to New York. It is hard to grasp the understanding or mindset of what was going on in those times, but I do say this - I want to feel that my mother loved me in her own way as I love her in my own way. Our bonding was short lived, so the relationship we shared was quite different from that of a child who remains with his mother from birth. Through it all, nothing can replace the bond of mother and child and alleviate the pain caused by the absence of a father.

As the weather began to break from the bitter cold days of winter and my mother had healed from giving birth to me, the city was still calling her back. She yearned to return to work and to the place she had grown to love, New York City. Perhaps it was to reunite with you, Dad, and to give you the news of having a son. I do not know, but living in McBee was not something she was interested in doing. Grandma wished her well and vowed to take care of me if she wanted to go back to New York, but it was understood that I was not leaving with her, and I was staying with my grandmother. In early March of 1966, she returned to New York. My grandmother recalled that by the time my mother returned to South Carolina I was walking, maybe nine months to a year after she returned to New York. This is how the timeline was put together to show she arrived somewhere around Christmas of 1966. There are many stories of the gifts she brought back for me and other family members when she returned. No one knows the reasons for my mother's return, but it was clear that something had gone wrong in New York, and she had made the decision never to return there. It's only my speculation that the relationship with you did not turn out to be what she had expected.

Upon her arrival back to South Carolina, word traveled to the old flame she had from her days of working in the peach orchards before leaving for New York. She had been courted by Sunny from Cheraw, South Carolina, about 30 miles away from McBee. Rekindling of their relationship, they wasted no time, and within two months on February 6, 1967, they were married. This was considered an abrupt decision on her part, and yielded major consequences in years to come. They began their own family, and my sister, Sharon, was born shortly thereafter. In the beginning, they lived with my stepfather's parents, and that was one of the reasons given for me remaining with my grandmother. By the time they were settled into a home of their own, I had become very attached to my grandmother. It was decided (though I am not sure how mutual the agreements were between my mother and grandmother) that I would remain where I was, with my grandmother. There are memories of visits with my mother and fun times that I spent with her and with my other brothers and sisters though we lived apart. I was extremely happy with my grandparents. I was spoiled from birth, loved, and looked upon more as a son and little brother rather than as a nephew or grandson.

There were many times my grandmother would tell me this particular story. As I got older, one day she made a powerful statement. She informed me that the man I called my father married to my mother was indeed not my father at all. Surprisingly, it really did not bother me or so it seemed at the time. It never changed anything, because like you, my step-father was never around. The same respect I gave to my stepfather in the beginning,

I continued to give even after learning he wasn't my real dad. Frankly, Grandma would not have had it any other way. Anything becomes better than nothing. Although it was rare that my mother and step-father saw me, it was better than not being around at all, which is the route you chose to take.

It would be later one day in conversation that Grandma gave me more information about you, but that time it was different. I was nearly ten or eleven years old when there was a confession that affected me deeply. She asked me to understand her reasoning and her state of mind. She would go on to remind me of her mindset during those early days. She said, "I do not want you to harbor any hatred or ill will towards your father for not being in your life." In reality, at that time I had no feelings one-way or the other. I had not missed you, and besides there were so many uncles in my life along with my grandfather, I thought I had everything. Nevertheless, I asked her why. She said, because you never denied that I was your child. She informed me that you called shortly after I was born and offered to help with me and if she needed anything to let you know. At one point, you asked to visit, but she saw that as a threat of losing me forever, and to her that was not an option. She admitted she told you– "You better not ever set foot in my yard, and if you do, I will kill you." Obviously, she was quite persuasive. As was the case when she dealt with most people, folks took her at her word. She was quite convincing that she could not bear the thought of losing me in any way. "I prayed for you," she would say. She admitted it was not the right thing to have done, but at the time, she said it was all she knew to do to keep me. By her account, you never tried to contact her again. When I was almost a teenager, she tried to search for you. The information she had ended up creating more questions than answers. She realized she'd made a big mistake since I started to need more things that she couldn't quite provide as I grew older. So, Dad, I'm left to wonder if life would have been different if secrecy, self-gratification, and pain didn't camouflage the truth so many years ago. Dad, I'm not sure if my mother aided in my grandmothers' quest to find you, but I doubt it. I'm certain that if my mother ever wanted to reach you, she would have known exactly where to start looking, but my grandmother never found you, so I'm left to wonder.

There has been a great deal of speculation over the years as to why I never asked about you and why my mother never offered answers to the question. My position became this: She didn't have to ask who her father was, so why should I? I think her position was if I want to know I could ask her, but my mother wasn't going to volunteer the information. So, we were both stubborn to the core. I guess it's fair to say that neither of us wanted to deal with the hard reality of my beginning. By the time I was older and knew certain facts that could have major consequences if revealed, I was too afraid to upset my mother and felt it disrespectful to force her to talk since she didn't say anything, and did not want to cause issues with her husband, my stepfather Sunny, whom I have always called Dad, knowing he wasn't really my dad.

I can only assume that for my mother the emotions of what happened between the two of you remained very raw and were too painful for her to discuss. I respect and love my mother too much to ever go there; instead, I waited for the right time, but that right time never came. Its funny how you always think there will be enough time to know the truth. But then, time is the one thing over which we have no control. I have learned to never put off for tomorrow what you can do today. The longer you wait the harder it is to find closure if you are ever fortunate enough to get to that point in your life. Find closure early, or you will destroy yourself with resentment, anger, and blame in the process. So, Dad, I waited and waited. I waited for you to show up; I waited to ask my mom about you; I waited to find you, and time ran out. Mom died early after suffering from MS, so we never got the chance to talk honestly about you or why things went the way they did. I remain haunted by the call I missed from her on the day she died. That day, I can't remember exactly what I was doing, but I was busy doing something routine, and my phone rang. As I looked at the caller ID, I thought I'll get this later and call them back later, not knowing who exactly was calling, just one of the family. That evening my phone rang again, and I decided to answer. My sister told me Mom had passed away earlier. She explained my mother had called everyone that day before she passed. I realized then that the phone call I ignored had been my mom. The first thing that popped in my mind was she was calling to tell me those things about you she had not said all these years. It was like I lost both parents in the same moment. I lost her, but I had lost you since she was the only one that could possibly tell me about you. I think she knew the end was near and wanted to set the record straight and to tell me who you were, but now I'll never know. One thing is for certain: we all live by choices and often the consequences of those choices we make force us onto different paths and to sometimes make better choices.

As I share this letter with you, I want you to understand that your absence has resulted in years of *invisible pain*. As I search for the courage to peel back the layers of pain and anguish, I find that this is more of a daunting task to reveal the "true me" even to myself. Dad, for years I have refused to take ownership of who I am, where I came from, and why I felt ashamed. When my mother died, a door closed to finding these answers. Understand that when you have been pretending for most of your life, finding reality and expressing it openly is difficult and, a real challenge, when pride has always been proven to be your worst enemy.

Anthony

DAD, THESE ARE MY MEMORIES OF LIFE ON THE FARM AND LIVING IN THE SOUTH.

THE MCLEOD FARMS HOME PLACE HOLDS more memories for me, because I remember being surrounded by acres of peach trees for miles on end. There were orchards far as the eye could see. I met my first child-hood friends, Gin and Brenda, who also lived on the farm. They lived in the white house along the railroad tracks, and the large patch of pine trees between our house became our playground. Their father, Mr. Rich, also worked on the farm. We lived in the little red house at the end of the dirt road just beyond the pine trees. As with the house on Horton Place, there was not much to this house either. To get to the house, you would come off Highway 1 at the farm. The overpass goes over the railroad tracks, and along the side of the overpass is the road that leads to the house. I remember the house well, small but better than the other houses; however, that was not saying very much. Some of the floorboards I remember had holes large enough that you could see the ground. There was little indoor plumbing. The major upgrade was the sink in the kitchen that had a water faucet.

In the backyard of this house, my grandparents had pigs and a garden. That was what they did because of not having the means and resources to go to the store for meat and produce during the cold winter months. A true "green thumb", my grandmother was known for her many beautiful flowers no matter where she lived. It was as if anything she touched just seemed to thrive and grow so beautifully. She planted flowers around the front and sides of the house to add color and to beautify the clear patches of sand.

She often would say, "A house is not complete until the yard is filled with beautiful flowers." She worked hard to make this feel like home and another step closer to bringing more stability and independence for our family.

There were so many creative aspects to her. She was an extremely good seamstress, too. She had an ability to look at something someone was wearing and make it. She made many of her own clothes as well as the clothing for her daughters and many others in the community and our church. Cooking, however, was her specialty. She could always be found in the kitchen baking the best cakes and pies. All of her brothers and sisters would often show up for her great dinners. Although she had fewer means than most of them, I can never remember a time when family came home and she did not prepare a great dinner. I have never gone to bed hungry, nor awakened hungry without a meal provided. I'm not saying it was always what I wanted to eat, but there was always something to eat. My creative ideas in the kitchen, and my love for cooking without a doubt came from standing beside my grandmother at the stove. I watched everything she did, as she would often say: "You must learn to cook for yourself, there's nothing wrong with a man cooking". Men didn't cook back then, so this is where I found the desire to cook and to exceed in culinary school, Dad. Everything that was an interest to my grandmother became an interest for me. My grandmother had a love of flowers, and now do I. She loved to cook nice big meals for her family, so I love to cook when entertaining. My uncles liked nice, clean cars, so do I. You weren't there, Dad, to teach me and for me to learn from your examples, so I learned from all the other people around me. What might I have learned from you?

Around 1970 and 1971, I was put in the Head Start program that was held on the outskirts of town in a white house surrounded by big trees. I remember Ms. Cannon was the teacher, and she would make her rounds picking up children that did not have transportation in her car and taking us to school. In the afternoon, she would do the same to ensure that every-one was home safely and dropped me off at Grandma's. I have fond memories of learning so many songs, as well as numbers, the alphabet, and very basic reading. The most memorable thing, I can recall is my graduation from Head Start. There was a stage performance. Lisa and I were selected to perform the Hokey Pokey as part of the graduation ceremony. We put our left foot in and our right foot out and shook it all about. It was one of the most popular songs of the time. The two of us acted out our skit as the audience of parents and friends sang along with such cheer and excitement. I was a bit shy at the time, so my performance was quite reserved to say the least; however, my grandmother was there to cheer me on. Shame on you for not being there to enjoy and support your son.

The ride home from the graduation is quite memorable as well. As usual, we would ride with our close family friends, Mr. Lester and Ms. Katie, since we did not have a car. Sitting in the back seat was my grandmother, my aunts, Jackie and Mildred, and myself. Mr. Lester began to comment on my performance as he often gave his opinion on various matters that he deemed would be beneficial for someone to be and do better. Although complimentary, he was not at all happy with the way I handled myself on stage. He would go on to tell me to never hold my hand in front of my face or my mouth and never look down at the floor when in front or when talking to people regardless of what color they were. Regardless of being afraid or nervous, this was always unacceptable. "Son", he said, "always carry yourself with pride regardless of your possessions." I never forgot that advice. As the years passed, I understand that, though the civil rights movement of the 1960s had come to somewhat of an end for some, it was only the beginning for many in the South. This was the real South, and he was teaching me at an early age to always have pride and to never feel intimidated or inferior to others regardless of their race or status. He said to always look a man in the eye without fear of retribution, because if you don't, they will always treat you as if you're nothing. This early lesson proved to be an important moment in my education, because in many respects I would find a true love for speaking in public. Indeed, I began to become quite bold from that day on. My grandmother always said these things to me; however, this was a man that I trusted and respected. When a man I respected told me something, I took it as Gospel.

Dad, I do recall a situation when we had to go to Chesterfield, South Carolina, for something. I must have been about 6 or so at the time, and there were two water fountains. I was thirsty and excited, so I took off running to get a drink. Most kids even to this day often take off running to the water fountain if one is in sight. I remember there was a big one and a small one. Of course, I wanted the big one and obviously had selected the Whites-Only fountain. My grandmother quickly ran over to me as this giant of a white man was coming towards me. I had no idea that I was doing anything wrong. This man, as I recall, appeared very red, his skin colored in anger. Pulling me away, I recall my grandmother saying to him she was sorry, but I didn't know not to use that one. I remember how she said it in such an apologetic way, as if she or I had done something that was morally wrong. This was quite strange for me; I had never seen my grandmother react this way before. As we went to the car and rode home, I recall her laughing about what I had done. She would often talk about that day, and in a way, she appeared to view that as a moment of pride. I did something that she wouldn't ever do. I understand looking back now that perhaps to that point she had never had the courage to drink from the fountain that had cold water in a public place. It's amazing to think of how angry people would get over a simple drink of cold water back then.

Dad, I also have a vague memory of going to the cotton field with my grandparents and getting lost in the field. She recalled my having a little croaker sack like everyone else. When I wandered off and got lost, hysteria was not the word to describe the terror we experienced that day. I was so afraid, and so was my grandmother until she found me. Everything stopped, and everyone began searching for me in that wide-open cotton field. Let's just say that when I was found I got a very good talking-to. I do not remember ever going to the cotton field again. I'm sure I caused them to lose money while searching for me, because you were paid by the pound and not the hour for the cotton you picked. After all, a huge cotton field is not the place for a kid under the age of 5 years old, but you did what you had to do to take care of children back then.

So, Dad, as you can see, I have always been protected and loved even in your absence. I understand that we are rich not by our assets but by our values. Perhaps you never thought of how life was or has been for me, but I've learned how to survive and how to live without you. Could things have been better with you? Perhaps not. Perhaps so. I may never know. What I do know is that at an early age I learned the value of hard work. My grandparents really toiled in those cotton fields.

Sincerely,

Anthony

DAD, INDEPENDENCE AND FREEDOM COME WITH SACRIFICE AND HARD WORK.

IN EARLY 1971, MY GRANDMOTHER SAID she could no longer live on the cotton and peach farms under someone else's rule. Not that the McLeod's were cruel, but she simply had enough of living in someone else's house under their rules and their power. She had been dealing with this for years from one farm to another, and she decided it was time to move. She told my grandfather that she wanted her own home. She wanted her own independence, her freedom, and control of her own destiny. She said, "My independence would only come when I have the keys to my own house." My grandfather was not as ambitious as she was, so if this was going to happen, she was going to have to make the first move.

Working on the farm, mostly seasonal, did not qualify as a real job or permanent employment in the eyes of most homebuilders or banks. She approached C.M. Homes, a company that at the time was building homes in stages depending on the amount of money you had or the amount of credit you were approved or qualified for. This company would agree to build the house under certain terms and conditions. Someone would have to find a permanent job, make sufficient income, open a bank account, and come up with the down payment. It was decided that my grandfather would continue to work on the farm in order to provide shelter. Someone had to work on the farm to live in order for us to live in the house, and my grandmother would look for a better paying job. Since her education was better, and in fact my grandfather only had skills for working on the farm, my grandmother was the one to venture out and look for a job.

31

Soon, she found employment cutting chickens at a poultry plant in Hartsville, South Carolina, the closest shopping town about 14 miles away from McBee. My grandmother would describe in great detail the hard work involved in cutting chickens rapidly in the freezing-cold ice water, but she did so for almost two years in order to buy her own home. She would often talk about how her hands would hurt, how it would take hours for the numbness to wear off, and how by then it was time to start the process all over again.

She finally saved the $1,000 she needed for the down payment. She had been employed long enough to be considered as a permanent employee, thereby meeting the qualifications to build her house. However, there was still a slight problem. The land cost $500 an acre, and she had to have a deed to the land in order to begin construction. She was $500 short of that goal and had no clue where the money would come from or how many more months she would have to work to save it.

One Saturday, I remember while we were visiting Great-grandma, my Great-grandmother began to ask about how much money my grandma needed to get for her new house. My grandmother was a woman of pride and never wanted to burden her own mother and did not consider asking her for help. Great-grandma lived alone and had bills of her own, so asking was never considered an option. That's just how she was, but her mother had other plans. Great-grandmother wanted her daughter off the farm and into her own home - and she was willing to sacrifice to see it happen and gave her the $500. Surprised and happy, my grandmother was finally on the road to her independence, and was so extremely grateful and thankful. So just like that, God stepped in and made a way out of an impossible situation. So, my great-grandmother, Eliza, purchased the land for my grandparent's home and helped pave the road to a better life eventually for me.

The land ironically was purchased from the McLeod family that owned the farm where my grandparents worked and lived, an acre lot just outside of the town limits about two miles down Highway 151 in a little section called Tony Hill. The final plans were completed, and construction had finally begun on our new home. My grandparents, aunts, and uncles worked their jobs during the day and in the evenings and weekends continued to put the finishing touches on the new house. There would be three bedrooms, one full bath, a living/dining room, and a kitchen. Because this was a "stage builder" and there was such a small budget, the builder only completed the bare basics of the house in order for my grandparents to gain a certificate for occupancy. The builder framed the house and put on the standard siding and painted the exterior. The floors were installed and ceilings dry-walled. There was a hot water heater and a few standard kitchen items although there was no budget for wall cabinets. The bath had plumbing fixtures, and the electrical work was in place. There was no insulation, but my grandparents had managed to find enough money to panel the main areas of the house. However, to provide privacy in the bedrooms, they had to get creative. They broke down large boxes from the local mill and nailed the panels to the studs. There was no money for interior doors, so sheets were used. Even though there was no running water at first, this was indeed far better than anything we ever had before. A wood stove for heat was in the living room area and that basically finished off the space.

On December 24, 1972, at the age of 7, I witnessed the celebration of my grandparent's independence. They embraced home ownership for the first time in their lives. The Outen family loaded up Mr. Lester's old truck and left a lifetime of living in borrowed houses on various farms in the past for their own home. This was truly a new beginning, and it was an extremely busy day. Not only was this their personal "Independence Day", but it was also Christmas Eve. I can remember running around playing with my cousins Junior and Tony as the house was being arranged. We were quite the characters. We were always getting into something, always paying the price for breaking the rules or just plain being bad. We really didn't know any other way to be. I never realized until much later that I could own a house as a young man and gain that independence that early. Even my uncles in their late twenties were still living at home. So, when I was in my twenties, it took a young co-worker to ask me why I was renting an apartment when I could easily buy a house like she had. I didn't know I could go to the bank and get a loan for a house. I thought I wasn't old enough. I was in the city, but my mind was still in those old southern rules my grandparents lived by.

One of the memories I had about Grandma's first house was the clean tan floor of the kitchen. That great feeling of being somewhere nice and pretty. New door, nice windows, painted cabinets. Everything was so clean.

On this day, I recall the first thing my cousin, Tony, Junior, and I had to eat were mayonnaise sandwiches with Kool-Aid to drink. Tony could make a song out of anything. He even had a song for a ketchup sandwich which we loved to eat. I remember it well, because we sat in a semi-circle on the kitchen floor as my aunts, Jackie and Mildred, prepared lunch for us. This was memorable, because we had never sat on the floor to eat before. The floors in the other homes were so dirty and worn, and my grandmother would never allow us to sit to eat that way. We loved mustard, mayonnaise, and ketchup sandwiches. Finding meat for those sandwiches was rare. It's hard to imagine and reflect on some of the things I used to eat as a kid, but I realize now that there were many people who had less to eat and for some nothing at all. I don't recall there being a Christmas tree even though it was that time of year. That's not to say that there wasn't one, but with all of the work going on, I can't imagine my grandparents finding the time to get a tree and decorate it. I do remember having lots of Power Wheels and Tonka trucks to play with on Christmas morning. You know, I never thought about how you were never there to give me presents, because they gave me what I needed.

In the summer, Granddad would place these huge barrels at the corner of the house to catch rainwater for bathing. Because there was no well for running water, we would go through the woods to our Cousin Rea's house. They had a faucet on the front porch and were always generous. I can still remember carrying those 5-gallon buckets and gallon jugs back and forth throughout the day on the winding path through the woods leading to her house. This was how my dirty cousins and me would wash at the end of the day. Grandma made lye soap, and I guess that was good; otherwise, we would have never gotten clean. Getting as filthy as we could in the dirt seemed to be acceptable. There was no escaping the dirt and clay; it was everywhere. When the barrels of rain water were dirty we would dump it and wait for more rain. Although not your typical bath, these were not typical times, and to us it seemed normal. Just writing about this in a letter to you it all sounds so primitive, but it is the way things were back then and really not so many years ago.

In August of 1973, Uncle Sammie returned home from boot camp. He had joined the army to make some major changes to better enhance our living conditions. He had a pump and water well installed with all of the necessary plumbing to ensure that water was flowing into the house before he left for his next tour of duty in Germany. We finally had running water, and for the first time, I didn't have to carry water anymore. We entered "modern civilization" with that well and pump.

You probably never experienced anything like that living in New York City, Dad, but what seems primitive now was normal back then. I don't feel these were painful memories, because certainly they weren't. These are some of the most treasured moments of my life, and at times, they bring me back to reality of sacrifice and true endurance. I must say that without the experiences and guidance of the wonderful men and women of the communities where I was raised, I wouldn't have the reflections on life that I do. So, Dad, I must say, you owe many in McBee, South Carolina, a great deal of gratitude and thanks for being there and doing the things that you should have been there to do.

Love,

Anthony

DAD, COUSIN REA'S HOUSE OFFERED ADVENTURE, CREATIVITY, AND DISCOVERY.

EVERY NEIGHBORHOOD KID WOULD ASSEMBLE IN Cousin Rea's yard from the time we woke up until it was time to go to bed. She had so many children and grandchildren; it was fun to have more people to get in trouble and play with. Besides climbing the large chinaberry trees in Cousin Rea's yard which we did often, there were hundreds of wild plum trees and blackberry patches simply everywhere. We would walk the dirt roads to the plum trees, and there we would stay for hours, climbing, eating, and having fun. We even ate something called "sour weeds". I'm not sure I would try it now, but they were quite tasty and bitter. It never crossed our minds that we were probably surrounded by snakes and other dangers as we went about plundering through old barns and abandoned houses looking for what we called treasure. Perhaps that is a part of the problem with kids today - they stay in the house all the time and never learn to explore and discover things that were not invented by someone else.

Because there was so little money, we would make our own toys. One of our favorite pastimes was rolling cans. This was how it worked: We would go to the trash, find 12-ounce drink cans, fill them with sand, and pack them tight. We would then put foil in the top opening to keep the sand from coming out, and that was our coolest toy. We would then roll the can down the road to see whose can would go the furthest or do the coolest tricks on the curved dirt roads. We truly amused ourselves with everything from sticks we made into toy guns for playing Cowboys and

Indians to playing Hide-and-Seek. There's a lot you can do with your imagination when your imagination is all you have.

Another pastime was sitting on buckets along Highway 151 playing "name and claim that car." The game was simple. We all sat in a line, and each car served as a turn. When your car came, you really hoped for a cool car not a jalopy, an old beat-up car that no one wanted. The cool car that would give you the most points were Trans Am's, Corvettes, or any sports car for that matter. Whoever had the highest number of cool cars was declared the winner.

The summers brought even more new faces and new friends. Almost everyone in the community had grandchildren who lived out of state and would visit for long periods of time in the summers. Can you imagine having that many kids screaming and yelling in your yard all day, Dad? One thing for sure, we knew that we wouldn't dare get out of line. In those days, if you did something wrong, you would get your rear tanned on the spot, then they would tell your parents, and you would get it again. No such thing as "Don't tell my children what to do." or "Don't spank your child."

Dad, I've always been one to find adventure in everything. I'm not sure if I get that from you or not, but it is who I am. I've learned to appreciate the little things, because those are the things that in the end will sustain you. From the tin can to the plastic buckets on the side of the road, each offered hope. I could have easily been taught to sit by the road and be a bum, but I was not. I learned that if you just believe in the power of prayer and yourself, one day the bitter taste of a sour weed in South Carolina can be a sweet reminder for the great things I have now.

Anthony

DAD, MY EARLY SCHOOL YEARS WERE QUITE ADVENTUROUS.

I REMEMBER RUNNING AWAY WHEN I was in elementary school, but I didn't runaway like most kids do. It all started in Ms. Rose's second grade class. Ms. Rose was a wonderful teacher, very strict but in a loving and God-fearing kind of way. She loved music. Ms. Rose was the only teacher in the school allowed to have a piano in her classroom, and she always made great use of it.

The day always started with a prayer in school, the pledge of allegiance, and often a song while she accompanied us on the piano. The songs were often old Gospel hymns and would never be allowed in today's public schools. There were never any complaints, and there were days others joined in on the singing. Some mornings, you could hear her singing and playing in her classroom as we got off the bus. Of course, it didn't hurt having Mr. Evans as the principal; he was also an ordained minister. One of the favorite songs she would play and have us sing was *Go Tell it on the Mountain.* We sang this song so much until one could say it was the anthem of McBee Elementary. This song was most popular at assemblies, especially during the Christmas season.

Ms. Rose was quite strict, but it was in her class that I remember learning to read. She placed great emphasis and significance on our knowing how to read aloud. She would make you read repeatedly until she was satisfied that you had done your best, and even then, you still had to read some more. If I had to guess, I would say reading was always priority number one in her class. She would often say: "Children, if you don't learn to read, you will never succeed. I'm here to make sure you succeed. Now get to it."

This was not to say that her class was a cakewalk by any means. Any time you got out of line, which I often did, she had no problem bringing you right back. Yes, I lived in the time of classroom discipline in which teachers didn't ask for respect but insisted upon it. You were told what to do not asked to do it, and it was expected to be done. Anytime you decided you wanted to do otherwise, there was always a yardstick or a nice ruler to help you see that your way really didn't matter. The classroom belonged to the teacher not the students. I can never recall a parent challenging the authority of a teacher or recall parents coming to the defense of any out-of-order student.

But I went too far with Ms. Rose and Mr. Evans, the principal. One day, a class friend, Bob, and I decided that we wanted to be class clowns and not pay attention to our teacher. After countless call downs and licks, we still didn't seem to get the message. I have no idea what I could have possibly been thinking. Ms. Rose was so upset and frustrated that she told us that we weren't going to be allowed to eat lunch that day as punishment. She told us to sit and eat our fingernails, but I didn't get the joke, and I took her seriously. Besides, I wanted to eat lunch. This was a major deal, because I always looked forward to lunch. Food in the cafeteria then was real home cooking not processed food.

Not being able to have lunch was such a devastating thought to me that I decided I would come up with my own plan to eat lunch. My plan with Bob was that we would run away to the high school and eat lunch there. I told him that my aunts, Jackie and Mildred, were students in the high school and that they would take us to lunch so we could eat. I was very serious about eating lunch. The second grade class lined up, the bell rang, and Ms. Rose, true to her word, refused to let Bob and me line up. She told us to sit there and be quiet until the rest of class returned from lunch. As the class left, we made our move, but Bob got cold feet and refused to leave with me. As usual, if I had a plan, I rarely backed down. For that stubbornness, I would often pay the price, this time was no exception. Although the high school was a little over a mile away from the elementary school, I was determined to make a run for it.

I made my move, so I peeped around the corner to see if the coast was clear; it was so I ran for the side door. Once out of the door, it was a bee-line across the road and through a path in the woods as fast as I could go. Eventually, I came out of the woods and onto the main road, finding my way to the high school a mile away. I'm not sure how long it took me, but I do remember constantly looking back and being mad at Ms. Rose, because I wanted my lunch.

Upon arriving at the high school, I had no idea where to go or what to do next. I remember looking up the many steps that led up to at the three sets of double doors. As I began to climb to the top of the stairs, I went into what seemed like the largest building I had ever seen. Once in the hall, I knocked on a classroom door, and a teacher came out and asked, "Who are you? What are you doing here?" I replied, "My name is Anthony Outen, and I'm looking for my aunts, Jackie and Mildred, so that I can eat lunch." That's just what I told her verbatim. I then went on to inform her that my teacher, Ms. Rose, would not give me any lunch at my school, so I had left to come there.

The teacher then pulled me by the hand and brought me into the class-room. She asked if anyone knew whom I was. The town being so small, everybody knew everybody. Sure enough, Glenda, a neighbor and friend of my aunts, held up her hand. She knew me. Glenda asked me again what I was doing. I repeated to her why I was there. I wanted lunch. The teacher told Glenda to take me to the office. *"To the office?"* I thought, *"Wait, what about lunch? I came all the way here for lunch not to go to the office!"* I even didn't get to see my aunts. Now, I suddenly realized that things certainly weren't going to end up with me eating lunch and sneaking back into elementary school and into Ms. Rose's classroom without a problem. It was beginning to look very bad. I had a plan to get to the high school, and I got there, but I didn't have a plan to get back to Ms. Rose. But I was soon about to find out.

As the principal put me in the car and drove me back to the elementary school, I was met at the door by the full wrath and fury of Ms. Rose. She was steaming. If I thought I had plucked her nerves in the classroom, I was about to find out what it was like for her to blow a gasket. She was scared of what could have happened to me, but it was the anger that was showing. Let's just say it was not a good thing to have done that. She pulled me into her classroom and wailed on me there first. Then she dragged me to see Mr. Evans. He was a strong giant of a black man with a deep voice, even deeper than Barry White. Just to hear him say, "Good morning," made you almost want to cry with fear.

There was a seat beside his desk, also known as the hot seat, and in the corner behind his desk was the "equalizer", which some may simply call the paddle. I don't remember everything he said, but I know he was going to let me have it. I was still in tears from my recent encounter with Ms. Rose's ruler that she used. This was now the moment of truth, the meeting of the minds with Mr. Evans. I don't remember the number of licks with the paddle I received, but trust me, it was enough for me never to have any bright ideas like that again. Although they pinned a note to my shirt for my grandmother to find out about my misadventure, she already knew before the bus stopped and let me off that afternoon. So did all the other kids in the neighborhood. I remember her words, "Go right out there and get me a switch." It didn't matter I'd already had two whippings. From then on, I knew better than to misbehave in Ms. Rose's class or runaway ever again.

It's amazing to think back on those days without asking myself "Did you, Dad, ever do anything like that before?" There must be some stories that you have that could answer these questions for me. You can see that even as a kid I would go even if I had to go by myself and handle the consequences if they arose. I guess you could say I have always been going after something, someplace, or someone from a very young age. Your son is strong, not by your guidance and support, but from your inability to perform the paternal duties. I pray that one day you will find the courage to face and recognize the son you pretended didn't exist by your actions, remaining *invisible* to me for so many years as I face up to situations in my life. What would you have done, Dad, in my place?

Your Son,

Anthony

DAD, MY FIRST CRUSH AND MY FIRST LOSS CAME EARLY.

DAD, TO GIVE YOU A GLIMPSE of events of my life, I find it imperative to share the many little details that may seem insignificant now but were so critical for a father to be a part of them. It's important for you to realize the many things you missed out on during your absence. You didn't meet my third grade teacher, Ms. McMillan, or know how she taught me how to write neatly. You didn't set any standards for me, but there were so many that stood in the gap for you and did just that. It was in her class that I developed my first crush, and it was her that helped me and the other students to cope with the realities of life and death, something you weren't there to do.

Like Ms. Rose, she was a very tough teacher. She was never accepting of what she called "chicken scratch". She required everyone to continuously trace the alphabet in print and in cursive until she was satisfied, and this was not often. She didn't care if our hands ached or not; she only wanted and only accepted perfection. Eventually, I got it, and I developed a love for writing neatly. To this day, I receive many compliments on my handwriting, and I owe that all to my third grade teacher.

A very sad and devastating event changed our class and even the school that year. This was the first and only time I ever experienced the loss or death of a classmate. Being a student of a small school and a small town, everyone was very close. What affected one person, for the most part, affected everybody. As with most kids, there would be the passing of love letters that read, "Do you like me? Check yes or no." Depending on the day, you may get "yes", although it only lasted for a few minutes. It was just puppy love. There were about 10 girls in the whole third grade. In the morning, it was Donna. By third period, it was Lisa, and so on. Well, Donna was for a while considered my girlfriend although neither of us knew what that meant. I'm sure you would have found humor in watching me experience puppy love for the first time. It's even funny to think about today as I write you. Did you ever think about what I must have been going through at all during that time? Did you ever wonder what I felt as a young kid? It just really seems perplexing to me how a man can walk around knowing they have planted a seed and never feel as though they need to water it for it to grow and survive. I wonder, Dad, why is that? You have missed so much, and this is only the beginning.

Sadly, one day, Donna was riding her bike, she fell, and she broke her leg. Although sad, it didn't seem that bad when we first heard about it. To show support, the school allowed the class to walk to Donna's house to see her. I was so excited; I had never been to her house before. I remember it well. We lined up in single file for the walk that was about 1/2 mile one way. There was a teacher in front and one in the rear to watch and guide our class. There were no concerns back then for students taking such a walk. We were happy to be granted time to visit our friend. Her house was a straight shot from the school.

As we all eagerly walked down the road, anxious to see Donna, we finally arrived at her house. Our arrival was announced at her door, and we entered a few at the time. Donna was sitting in her chair in a gown and a robe and her leg elevated on something that placed her cast in full view. She didn't have a lot to say, and she looked the same. The visit was so much fun. While I wasn't sure if she still considered me to be her boyfriend, I wouldn't dare ask. Each of us had the opportunity to sign her cast, and then we were on our journey back to school. It was such a beautiful day; I can remember it as if it was yesterday. I was so happy to have seen my girlfriend.

To my surprise, a few days later I was given some of the most devastating news. My friend, Donna, had died. How could this be? She had only a broken leg, and I thought that she would be back to school soon. But Donna's leg had become infected with gangrene. By the time it was detected and treated, it was too late. The deadly infection ended up taking her life swiftly. Many tears were shed that day, and you can only imagine the pain her family must have been experiencing. The funeral arrangements were made, and I was informed of the date and time. I wanted to go even though I hated going to funerals, but this was not just any funeral. It was Donna, and she was loved by everyone.

Once again, Dad, you weren't there to comfort my pain, or help me when clearly your presence could have made such a difference. I was unable to attend the funeral because of another man's failure to do as he promised. My grandparents didn't have a car, so I had to depend on others to get from place to place. I was promised a ride to the funeral by Sam, a close family friend and at the time also the school custodian. He promised me that he was going to the funeral, and I could ride with him, so I didn't make any other arrangements. I was certain he would come through on his promise. I remember coming home and putting on my only suit and dress shoes and then waiting. As the minutes ticked away, I became restless as I stood looking up dirt road waiting for his car to come over the hill, but it never did. My grandmother, feeling sorry for me, came out to tell me that I might as well change my clothes. She simply said, "It looks like you're not going." I didn't want to believe her, but her words were correct. She apologized although it was not her fault. I remember when she came out and talked to me and said, "You might as well take your good clothes off," and she made me change and hang my suit back up in the closet. I couldn't understand why at the time, but she simply said to me, "One day, you will have your own. When you have your own *and only* when you have your own, can you be certain of anything." I only wanted to at least say *Goodbye* to a friend, and couldn't even do that. The next day, I had to face all my friends that were there. It made me feel embarrassed. But it was just one of those moments why does this always happen to me? Why do people let me down? I didn't think of you, on that day Dad, but looking back, I'm glad my kids don't worry about that. My kids have had friends die, and there is no question, you just take them to the funeral. But the weird thing is I immediately think back to this particular memory and realize there are those things I don't want to, but I do anyway for my kids, because I know how it felt when I wanted someone to be there for me. Dad, I should have never had to depend on another man to do what was your responsibility. You failed me, and you failed yourself as a man. I write these words now to you not out of disrespect or anger, but only for you to see that it's not the big things that matter, it's the small things. Being a father is the gift that's suppose to keep on giving, not just throwing seed in the pasture and never checking to see the quality of the fruit.

I arrived at school the next day, humiliated and embarrassed. Everyone wanted to know why I wasn't there, but all I could say was I didn't have a ride. Class went on, but it was never the same. It took quite some time for things to get back to normal. It seemed that everyone really missed Donna so much. I know for certain that I did. I experienced *invisible pain* not only from the loss of Donna but from your failure as a father and my disappointment in a man I depended on because you were nowhere to be found.

Sincerely,

Anthony

DAD, THE POWER OF MUSIC DISCIPLINED ME AND GAVE ME THE STRENGTH TO LEAD.

I ALWAYS HAD A FASCINATION WITH music. My Aunt Freda had given me a little AM transistor radio, and I listened to it from early mornings until it would lose reception at night. When given the opportunity to catch a glimpse of the shiny instruments, I was instantly captivated by the wonderful sounds they made. I wanted to be a part of that, so when the band teacher visited our school I was eager to meet him to express my interest in band and music in general. You started music lessons in elementary school in order to be in the high school band later. We were given the opportunity to hold instruments for the first time. Each instrument was explained in detail so that we could decide what we wanted to play. What really caught my attention was the shiny snare drum that was on display. I loved that sound, and quickly decided that this was the instrument for me. There was one unexpected catch. The drum wasn't free.

After I was given all of the information about the cost, the classes and so forth, I couldn't wait to get home to share the news with my grandmother. As I began to tell her about it, I handed her the package the band director gave me. She looked at it, and said, "Anthony, do you know how much this stuff is going to cost?" I had no real idea; I just wanted to play in the band, and I had no understanding of whether or not we could afford it. I said that I needed to learn now if I wanted to be in the marching band when I went to high school. She politely said, "Anthony, I do not have the money to buy this expensive drum or pay the cost to rent one. You'll need to choose something else, and one day maybe I can get you into the band but not now. Times are too hard." To say the least, I was devastated, but life went on. I always kept the band and that shiny snare drum in the back of my head and believed one day there would be music in my future.

So much later, in high school, I still had never played an instrument. When I was approached by some friends in study hall, they told me there was a new band teacher, and he wanted more members for the marching band. I had already given up hope to join since I was so many years behind in instruction and still no drum. I couldn't read music and had no clue if I could make any contribution. Our small band needed people, and so none of my problems mattered. I went to Mr. Pierce, the band teacher and asked if I could join the band. He agreed, so I dropped study hall. I couldn't play an instrument, so I just sat in class until it was time to practice marching. I was given a melephone and told to just hold it and pretend to play it but don't try to play it on the field while I marched. There I was, marching around with a horn that I couldn't play. That was not going to hold my attention for long, but it did get me into the football games free and kept me busy, listening for the sound of the snare drum and the drum line in the background. I listened and watched every stroke the drummer would make. I studied his hands, how they moved around the drum, and how he made multiple sounds when he would strike different parts of the drum. I wanted to get closer and learn more. In order to do that, I had to become his friend. Drummers are very protective of their drums. During class, I began to sit in the back of the room with the drum section. I watched them play and listened to every sound. Memorizing those sounds became my refuge and the only thing that would keep me out of trouble and interested me in being in the band. The pretend melephone wasn't going to do it. I began to use my hands on the table as if I was playing the actual drum. Even at home, I was always tapping the songs on anything that made noise. In my head, it sounded like the snare, and I loved that sound, so I kept practicing the songs again and again with just my hands. I began to create new beats and memorized them all. The more I focused on the sounds, the more creative I became. After watching me practice my beats, one of the guys liked the sound and was kind enough to give me a set of his drum sticks. He taught me how to hold them, and until that point, it was the only instruction I ever received in band class.

There was only room for one snare drummer, and he was good. There was only one snare drum, and he played it. I stood no chance of getting on the drum line, but that didn't stop me from learning by ear every sound that came from that section. Even on the field when I was marching with the pretend horn I couldn't play, I was listening to the percussion section. At games, I watched the crowd and the cheerleaders' reaction to the sound of the drum line. I knew that was where I had to be. I asked Mr. Pierce if I could please learn to play the drums or anything in the percussion section, but he still said no. There weren't enough drums, and besides, he said: "You can't fake not knowing how to play a drum." I almost quit but continued to watch wait and listen.

Then, Dad, almost midway through marching season, there was an unexpected change. The snare drummer quit school or was expelled. I'm not sure what happened; I just knew he was gone. This was my only chance, but it was not going to be an easy sell to Mr. Pierce. Seeing the weakness of the band with no snare drummer, I decided it was now or never. After practice one day, I went into the instrument room where the drums were. The other band members were putting their things away, and I decided to try and play the school fight song on the snare. They didn't believe I could do it; I wasn't sure myself, but I was confident enough to try. I wasn't sure if the snare was still there, but it was. I began to play it just as I had memorized it from listening and watching during class. It must have sounded good, because Mr. Pierce came into the room and asked who just played it. At first I thought I was in trouble for playing the drums without permission, but that wasn't the case at all. When I answered, he just looked at me shaking his head and asked: "Who taught you how to play that? I thought you had never played drums." I said, "I learned by watching, listening, and practicing with my hands and a set of drum sticks on my spare time." He then said: "Play the whole thing from the top." I did, and continued to play every song by ear with no music. If I heard it once, I could memorize and play it again. Shaking his head and smiling, he looked at me and said, "I guess you're our new snare drummer." Just like that, I went from pretending to play a horn to a lead position on the drum line.

I now had something else to master and hold my attention. The more I practiced the better I became. I practiced so much until my hands would cramp and curl around the drum sticks. I began to create new beats, and the band loved it. The cheerleaders loved it as well. They often requested me to play something for them to dance to, and that's exactly what I did. I was in my element, and feeling great about myself. Although the lack of money in elementary school had stopped my dream for a while, I had been blessed with a new opportunity, and it didn't cost me anything. It's amazing how in God's own time He provides our every need. "What's for you will always be for you." This is what grandma used to always say, and it has proven to be true time and time again. On Friday nights, the sound of my snare became the marching cadence for the entire band. Though nervous at first, I pulled it off and never looked back. By the time the season was over, everyone loved my drum beats, and the small stadium rocked at every game.

As usual I wanted more. I began to watch band competitions and larger bands perform. This made me want the drum line to be bigger and better. I needed a larger percussion section, but the school was small, and there weren't many students interested in music. Most of my male friends weren't interested in band, so I focused on the girls. I knew I could get their attention long enough to at least hear me out. It was a long, hard process but I finally convinced Veronica to play the cymbals and Ann and my cousin Goose to play bass drums. None of them had ever played in the band before, but we practiced endless hours together. Every day we worked to create beats that people would love to hear. I moved to the marching quad drum set. I had become good enough to play multiple drums simultaneously. This proved challenging but very rewarding, and it definitely got me a lot of attention on and off the field. BJ started playing the snare drum, and this line would become the most dynamic drum line ever. BJ was the only one who had learned to read music and had taken band class. He held his own, and the rest of us learned how to read music somewhat, but most of the time we just listened to the band play first then created our own beats. When the band entered our first competition, we didn't win, but we weren't last. We received a quality performance award, and that was a major accomplishment for a band the size of most schools' color guard teams.

The band kept me focused and for the most part out of trouble. Mr. Pierce gave me the opportunity to be creative and entrusted me to recruit my own percussion section. He didn't have to do that, but I guess he saw something in me that I didn't see in myself. In a sense, he had put the backbone of his band in the hands of a boy that had never taken a music class and could barely read music. The only thing I had was my will and motivation to succeed. The band was one more motivating factor to finish school. I may have easily fallen into the trap of absolute failure. My mind remained occupied with something positive besides drugs, alcohol or even worse. I remained effective and influential within the band and was voted band captain each year from that point on.

Dad, some of my family members had mentioned your music abilities, and perhaps that's where my desire and abilities come from. All I know is music made a change in my life, and maybe one day we can share musical stories of the days gone by.

Love,

Anthony

DAD, LESSONS OF A LEGACY CAME FROM BUILDING A CHURCH.

DAD, AS A CHILD, I OFTEN found myself in the midst of good men with great purpose. Many of the men of Shady Grove Missionary Baptist Church were an enormous influence on my life. Even though most of my morals and guidance came from strong women, it was a good thing that our little community was full of great role models that offered guidance and stability. Many of my days were centered around men of faith and strong spiritual beliefs. I'm not sure of your beliefs or what you stand for, but there must be something within you that made it possible for me to relate to people on levels that seem impossible to others.

Going to church while living in my grandparents' house was never an option or a choice, it was an expected requirement. My grandfather rarely went, but I don't recall a time when my grandmother didn't attend worship service. She made sure I attended Sunday school and made sure I did more than sit on the pew. It was mandatory to work in the church. It was understood that you will and you must give back for the many blessings God has provided for you during the week. Not from a materialistic standpoint, but in those days, most testimonies were not of monetary but of holistic thanks. Prosperity where I grew up was defined as *life, health, and strength.* Being thankful for having food for the family to eat, clothes on your back, and a roof over your head was a constant praise on Sunday mornings.

My earliest memories of Shady Grove were attending the little wooden church up on a hill down a clay road just past Tony Hill. The church was given a plot of land by the McLeod family which happened to be beside our new house. It would take several years for the church to be built. Block by block, board by board, I watched the construction of our new church, witnessing history in the making, although to me it didn't seem significant at the time. As a young child, I watched the few men, not a professional construction company, build the church from the ground up. The men who did a great deal of work in the early years were Rev. Backus, our pastor, Mr. Lester, Mr. Dave, Mr. Sam, and Mr. Cletus. My grandfather, Rufus, worked for a while helping with the floor and the roof. The congregation was so small that they could sometimes be counted on two hands, but they never stopped coming and working. They built a church that could easily seat over 300, but with only about 30 active members.

Mr. Lester, a deacon and a trustee at Shady Grove, lived just up the road from us and was instrumental in scheduling and arranging upcoming projects at the church. Because I was always hanging around him, I often found myself at the church site. He taught me the power of prayer and how to have faith when things looked impossible. On many occasions, the offerings would barely be enough to pay the pastor, but Rev. Backus never wavered in believing that the church would one day stand as a symbol of the power of God and the faithfulness of a few. He filled a void in your absence, Dad, and provided the spiritual guidance every young man needs in their lives.

Being around these men, watching them work diligently and faithfully build a house of worship gave me a foundation of hope, faith, and belief that there is honor in hard work and reward for the faithful. Everyone wore multiple hats to fulfill the vision. Our pastor was a master carpenter, so he did the plans and made sure the building was proper. To see him swinging a hammer during the week and preaching on Sunday mornings was proof that no man is above the people he is called to lead. Yes, he was the pastor, but his gift to build more than spiritual strength was the gift from God that was instrumental in uniting a community of believers.

Mr. Sam, the Sunday school teacher, also was the brick mason. When the work was too much for him, he would bring in a team of men to help carry out the duties. Mr. Lester and Mr. Dave filled in to do whatever was needed. They both assisted in everything from laying blocks to carpentry. Nothing seemed out of reach for them to do. My job was to run next door to our house and deliver ice water to quench their thirst from working in the sun on those hot South Carolina days. I would always find a way to do something; it didn't matter. What I always liked was to be around watching and learning.

It was through these men that I developed a passion to serve and to reach back to help mentor other young men that suffer from the *invisible pain* caused by invisible fathers. You, as well as other men that have walked away from their responsibilities as fathers regardless of the circumstances, are contributors to the society of angry, dysfunctional, and insensitive men. I've been blessed to have been among men of courage, rather than men of weakness. Dad, things could have gone the wrong way, and in some cases it did, but through it all I have survived. I often wonder if the part of me that is a survivor has ever had anything to do with you. One thing is for sure, as an absent father, you will never know what my life is like now.

Sincerely,

Anthony

DAD, WORKING STARTED WITH A BUCKET AND A DREAM.

AFTER SEEING MY GRANDPARENTS WORK HARD all their lives, I felt it was time for me to do the same. I wanted to work and help myself and the family. I had become bored sitting around the house doing nothing but cooking dinner and cleaning up the house for my grandmother. It was my responsibility to have dinner prepared and the house cleaned by the time my grandparents returned from work. I had been taught to cook anything in the kitchen by my grandmother, and she had no concerns leaving me home alone to cook dinner. Besides, the older boys worked the peach field and had a pocket full of change. I wanted that, too, and I could hang around them. My mind was made up, so I went to the local post office and completed the application for my social security card. I knew from listening to conversations that I couldn't get a job without one. Once the card arrived, I was ready to go to work. In South Carolina, you were allowed to work on the peach farms as early as 13. I didn't know what the job would entail, but I knew I was determined to try and do it.

One day while on the way to Hartsville with Mr. Dave, a deacon of the church, we passed Ridge Peach Farms. Both of my grandparents worked there. I asked him would he drop me off, because I wanted to get a job. He agreed, but with reluctance, because I had no clear plan on getting home. Actually, I had no idea but knew I could walk if I had to. Getting home was not my priority; I was interested in getting the job. I remembered my grandparents talking about the owner, Mr. DJ, so I knew he was the man

I needed to see. At the farm, I jumped out of the truck and walked into the office. I had no appointment, just was brave and determined to get a job. Sitting behind the desk was the secretary. I asked her if Mr. DJ was there, because I wanted to work. She hesitated from what she was doing and just looked at me. I was a short, skinny kid and weighed about 90 pounds soaking wet. Before she answered, in walked the tall and somewhat intimidating Mr. DJ with a cigarette in the corner of his mouth. He asked me, "What do you want?" Not exactly, the reception I was looking for, but I sucked it up and answered, "Sir, I want a job working in peaches. I'm 13 years old, and I have my social security card right here." I had to get it all in quickly, because he didn't appear to be someone that was interested in long conversations. He looked at me. "Who's your momma and daddy?" I told him my grandparents' name and told him that they worked for him. He said, "I think we have enough for now. Check back with me next year." Never one to give up, I then said, "But I don't mind working in the peach field picking peaches," just in case he was only considering me for working inside the pack house. I was determined to not take no for an answer for any job. He said. "Boy, it's mighty hot out there in that field. You're too small to be out there in a peach field in all that heat." I said, "I can do it, Mr. DJ." He looked harshly at me and took a big puff off of his cigarette as if I was getting on his nerves, which I'm sure I was, and said: "Alright, let's see if you can. Be here in the morning at 7:00am. Meet me across the street at the farm store ready to go to work."

I was so excited. I had a real job, and I must have run the whole way home. I took shortcuts along the way, because after all I had to beat my grandparents' home and get all of my chores done. Not to mention I had to convince my grandmother to let me work and explain how I was at Ridge Peach Farms in the first place. Always thinking, I decided to call in reinforcements. I stopped by Mr. Lester's on the way home to tell him the good news. If he was supportive, then I could say to her that Mr. Lester thought it was a good idea. Not that it would have changed anything, but at least, I had a plan. Mr. Lester also questioned my ability to work in the heat but said if my grandparents let me do it then I should try it. That boosted my confidence, so down the dirt road I went to do my chores and prepared to state my case when my grandparents came home.

About 5:30, my grandparents arrived home from work. Dinner was done, the house was clean, and I was eager to share my news. Finally, I got up enough nerve and said: "I got a job today. Mr. DJ said that I could come to work in the morning." They both looked at me at the same time. Let's just say she wasn't too happy with the news. She began to ask questions of how this came to be and said finally, "Look here, Anthony. I don't want you in a peach field, and that's that. It's too hot, and that peach fuzz causes your body to itch so badly. You stay here and work at the house. I'm going to pay these bills and get your clothes for you." Those words prompted a rare intervention from my grandfather. He rarely interjected his opinion or support on anything. However, on this occasion, he said, "Elizabeth, let the boy go to work if he wants to. It's not going to hurt him. Let him try it at least." I was shocked but glad that he came to my defense. That basically settled the discussion. Granddad had spoken, and for some reason, my grandmother yielded. I promised her I was still going to help with things around the house after work. Finally, after being worn down by both me and my grandfather, she agreed and laid down the law of how things were going to be. With that my first working days were just hours away.

The next morning my grandmother wanted to make sure I was wearing the proper clothes to the field. She gave me a straw hat and told me to drink plenty of water, because the temperature was going to be high. "Take your time, so you don't have a heat stroke, and do exactly what you're told to do. Don't talk back, and don't let me hear you're being grown. You hear me?" So many rules she would give, but if you wanted to do what you wanted to do, you must first listen to everything she had to say first.

I left early that morning with Granddad excited to go to work. My grandfather drove tractors from the field to the pack house. My grandmother worked in the pack house grading peaches. The pack house is the plant that sizes and processes the peaches from the field. There are multiple grading stages that they go through, which ultimately determines where the peaches will be sold and how much the peaches will cost. Working in the pack house was far better than working in the field.

That next morning, I arrived at the farm store, and I approached Mr. DJ to tell him I was ready for work. He looked at me and said, "Who are you?" My heart sank. I quickly reminded him about yesterday at his office and that he told me to be there. He then pointed at a green and white truck filled with men and said, "Go get on that truck and go with Mr. Q." So, I ran and jumped on back of the truck, and off I went to the field for my first day of work. I was the youngest person in the field, but that didn't matter to me. They gave me a peach bucket. I put it around my neck and started to work.

I was assigned to the same crew as my grandfather, and he kept a watchful eye over me all during the day. Since he would take the fresh picked peaches back and forth to the pack house, he often had time to stop at the store and pick up snacks and cold drinks for me. We had a great time together. Often he had a few minutes between trips to stand and talk. These were the best times I remember bonding with him. I didn't have to run to pick the peaches as the migrant workers did. They were extremely fast, because they were on production and were paid by the number of buckets they picked. I was an hourly employee, but that didn't mean I was given a free ride by any means. I was expected to work hard, and my age had very little to do with the expectations. My instruction was to keep a steady pace and remain busy. When my bucket was full, I would dump the peaches in the bin on the tractor. I needed to stay close to the migrant workers, most Puerto Rican, that picked the peaches but not get in their way. Mr. Q, the foreman of the field, was very nice and easy to work for. He liked my grandfather, and they would sometimes crack jokes during the day.

Dad, at the time I started working, the minimum wage was $2.65. To me, that was a lot of money. It was the same as my grandparents earned. No one made more than minimum wage, except the foremen and supervisors. I often worked a lot of overtime at peak season. We would often work six or seven days a week and up to ten hours a day. I took pride in working hard and adapted to the hot, itchy days of the peach field. My first paycheck was over $100.00, and I was so excited. It was my first time having that much money, and I couldn't wait to cash my paycheck. I went straight home to show my grandmother. I gave her my check stub and the cash, and in return, she gave me what she felt I needed as play money. I had no problems with that, because one of my main reasons for wanting a job was to help her. She would always tell me that winter was coming, and I wouldn't be working. "If you throw all of your money away now, you won't have anything to fall back on later." As much as I liked to spend money and still do, she was exactly right.

Working in peach fields was hard work, and there was nothing glamorous about it. The enormous heat, the itchy peach fuzz, and the flies and gnats were part of Character Building 101, because I was learning important life skills that have proven beneficial in my appreciation for honest work. I was taught that a man too lazy to work has no character or credibility. Since you weren't there, I learned them in the fields.

With Kind Regards,

Anthony

DAD, RISKY CHOICES CAN LEAD TO BAD CONSEQUENCES.

MS. WALKER OPENED MY EYES TO the world outside McBee. I enjoyed her class a great deal; she always kept it interesting. She was a woman who enjoyed international travel and would often return with many pictures and slides of her trips to Greece and other countries. It was exciting how she would bring the world to her classroom. Her class inspired me to want to see the world. She was a cool teacher, and she drove a classy sports car, a blue Fiat. The car was a two-seater with a tan interior. I loved that car. I thought it was just *so* cool. My other teacher, Ms. Gilliard, provided culture for her African-American students, and she instilled in us a sense of pride. She often reminded us of what she expected and tried her best to prepare us for the realities of high school. She would always tell us that she expected big things from us. She wanted us to always remember from where we came, no matter where we ended up in life. Her simple instruction and encouragement meant so much and often were motivating factors that kept hope alive.

But in spite of those teachers, I began to associate with much older guys after school which proved to be a recipe for disaster. I found it difficult to navigate those early pre-teen years. One summer, I let my curiosity get the best of me while hanging with an older crowd in our neighborhood. I got in way over my head. The local night club was called "The Blue Light". This is where we would all hang out during the day for drinks, snacks, pinball machines, and listen to the jukebox. I was too young to go in there at night, but they allowed younger kids during the day. There was a bench beside the club along the tree line of the dirt road, and this is where we would sit and play Spades. The teenage guys would sneak and smoke cigarettes, and we would crack many jokes. I started to smoke, too, and I did so until I was 18. I was more interested in hanging with the older guys than with children my own age. The word they called me in those days was "manish". It was slang for a kid acting grown up or thinking they were more mature than their real age. This was by no means a compliment. It was frowned upon to act out like this.

While sitting on the bench on a hot summer day, someone got the bright idea while the club was closed to reach in through the window and get some champale, a type of wine cooler. I must say that they didn't want me to have anything to do with it, but since I was there and might run and tell, they allowed me to stay to protect the secret. I kept bothering them to give me a taste. I had no idea what I was getting into but pleaded until they finally gave me a bottle. It tasted pretty good, very sweet, but soon that would change. A combination of things happened: the heat, the bologna and cheese sandwich with mayonnaise, and basketball. The next thing I remember was being home in my bedroom, sick and throwing up all over the place. My aunts, Jackie and Mildred heard me throwing up and came into the bedroom. When they smelled the alcohol, they left the room to tell my grandmother on me. I could hear them saying "Ma, Anthony's drunk." My grandmother told them to clean me up and the mess and got me into the bed to sleep off that terrible day. I only remember waking up for dinner. I was expecting a major beat down, but it didn't come.

My grandfather, who drank heavily and who rarely voiced his opinion about anything, was quite vocal with disappointment of me on that day. I was shocked, and I must say he really scared the crap out of me that day as indeed he should have. Then it was my grandmother's turn, and I really didn't know what to expect, but this is what she said. Dad, I will never forget her words. "Anthony, you see what drinking has done for your grandfather and some of your uncles, and now you want to get out there and act the fool with them. Well, I'm not having any of it." Then she said, "I really thought that you would have done better, because you know better. If that's how you're going to act, I'm going to stop sacrificing for you. I refuse to do the best I can by you and then have you throw it in my

LETTERS TO MY DAD

face. I'm disappointed in you, and one thing I won't allow to happen is for you to become a drunk in my house." With those words, the conversation ended. Honestly, she never said anything to me about it again nor did she bring it up when I made other mistakes. It was enough for me to know I had hurt her, and that is the last thing I ever wanted to do. For a long time, Dad, I felt ashamed of the day I hurt and disrespected my grandparents' home by coming in drunk after all they had done for me. I had to learn that everything is not always what it seems. Drinking does not make you an adult and will not change who you are, but it can change what you will become if you do not understand the consequences or aren't mature enough beforehand.

From that point on, I never came into my grandparent's house like that again. There are no highs worth losing the honor and respect of your loved ones. Even Mr. Lester, a man I always admired and respected, was disappointed in me that day. Through our many talks, he instilled and confirmed the fact that you do not need to drink to fit in. He often said, "A man will always lose the war if his ammunition is alcohol and not a sound mind. A clear mind will yield clear results. The drunken mind will only yield regrets and embarrassment. Falling when sober, you can stand again with dignity. Falling when drunk, someone else has to pick you up, and you display weakness and become a man who can never stand on his own, so the choice is yours." I still remember his words to this day.

Even with all of that support, Dad, following the rules and doing the right thing was becoming more rare than normal. Although McBee had a very small school, I learned rather quickly that big problems do not discriminate against small schools. I continued to want to hang with the upper classmen. I always found a way to connect with anybody regardless of their age, and often this came with major consequences and ultimately resulted in poor academic performance and rebellious behavior.

There were very few places to mingle in the school. There were designated smoking areas, but most of the guys I was hanging around smoked in the bathrooms. In order to smoke at school, you had to have a signed note from your parents on file in the office. Believe it or not, there were many approvals. Although I was experimenting with smoking, I was not crazy enough to ask for permission because then Grandma would have to sign the note, so I had to hide in the restrooms to smoke. My school breaks were split between hanging out in the restrooms smoking and in detention for my behavior. It was safer to get away with smoking in the old restrooms, because you had to go through two doors to enter. If we heard the first one open, you had time to quickly hide away your cigarette. Because the restrooms were always full of smoke, if you didn't get caught with it in your mouth or your hand, you were safe. Needless to say, many of us would get caught. For some reason, kids always think they are smarter than they are and that they are exempt from being caught doing something stupid.

In my desire to fit in coupled with the temptation to act out, I often found myself in the wrong place at the wrong time. Poor judgment put me into a position that literally scared me to death and was the one thing that got my attention and started me down a path of realizing that I had to find a way to do better and be a better person. At the beginning of the school year during football season, the coaches that teach classes would take the class to the football field as they prepared for Friday night's game. I remember this day, because the morning fog was extremely heavy, much more than usual. My cousin, Don, and I were just hanging out in the stadium seats while the coaches and a few student volunteers were on the field painting the lines. My cousin said he had a joint and wanted to know if I wanted to take a hit. I already was smoking cigarettes and was no stranger to being around weed. From time to time, I was known to smoke but never at school. For some reason, I decided, "What the heck, it's so foggy they won't see the smoke." We went down to the restrooms below the bleachers to fire up the joint. I had to use the restroom, and while washing my hands, my cousin got ready to light up and in walks Coach Uphill. I was at the sink, and Don was over in the corner. It happened so fast I had no time to respond. The coach walked straight to Don and asked. "What's that in your hand?" Don didn't answer. Although I had just used the restroom, I felt like I was about to wet my pants. Coach Uphill grabbed Don's hand, opened it and said, "Well what do we have here?" Don still said nothing, and we were off to the office. The short walk seemed to last forever as my mind was racing a million miles a minute. All I could think about was I probably have just lost everything, and my grandmother was going to kill me when I go home.

After interrogations in the office by Mr. Taker, the school principal, they sent me back to class but kept my cousin. I will forever be eternally grateful him. Don could have taken me down with him, because he didn't twist my arm and I went willingly to smoke weed although hadn't taken the first hit. Once again, always wanting to fit in and be popular, I had found myself in serious trouble and in compromising circumstances. Nevertheless, I was fortunate enough to escape the wrath of my grandmother, because my cousin chose to protect me instead of implicating me. His story was that I didn't know he had the joint and was innocent. Unfortunately, my cousin was expelled for the remainder of the school year, and I could have been too if not for his silence. The school didn't notify my grandmother of the incident, and I thought no one found out about me since I was not suspended or expelled. Later that day, Mr. Taker approached me in the hall as classes were changing and said: "Anthony, you are skating on very thin ice and it's only a matter of time before you fall in. I should expel you anyway, but I'm giving you a chance to straighten up and get your act together." All of a sudden, being cool and popular wasn't that big of a deal anymore. I made up my mind right then and there that I wanted nothing else to do with drugs. I never put another joint in my mouth. It wasn't worth it then, and it's not worth it now. There are two places drugs can take you: an early grave or behind bars - both are death sentences. I could have lost everything over a buzz that today I wouldn't even remember. I could have been expelled at the beginning of the school year like Don. I was willing to risk it all for a glimpse at the fast life. I am thankful that my actions on that day didn't bring hurt and heartache to my grandmother who was always there for me.

Sincerely,

Anthony

DAD, THESE ARE THE BEGINNING SIGNS OF AN INVISIBLE FATHER.

MANY OF THE SITUATIONS I FOUND myself in were from bad choices I made. Many times when things don't go our way, we look for someone to blame, but that's not what this is about. Did I have some bad breaks that were unfair and unjustified? Yes. Did I bring many of them upon myself? Very much so. We all have choices. Some choices are wise and some reckless. My way of thinking has always been rather complicated in nature, and I always wanted to do things a different way. I liked being able to do things no one else had done or that they couldn't do no matter how smart they were. I bored easily, and school simply bored me. I was not challenged then, and I lost interest. I developed the mentality to just get by, but that would prove to be one of the worst choices I could have made.

I was crying for attention, but it went unchecked and unnoticed. I was in denial, had low self-esteem, and felt shame. To me, my life simply wasn't good enough, and I felt as though I was missing something. There was no other love like that of a mother and a father. On most days, I felt like I had neither. Although my grandparents were great, they didn't fill that void. It was simply impossible, but everyone was under the sad illusion they were filling those voids for me. Dad, this is where you let me down once again. Can you imagine how I felt when I looked at the actions of other fathers with their sons and all I could do was pretend you existed and really cared for me? When I was around others that had both parents or at least one of them, it's hard for me with not to feel a sense of shame or inferiority. Do you think that was fair? I don't, but that's been the story of my life. It's easy to say it shouldn't matter much when you have known your parents all of your life, but when you haven't got them, it makes a world of difference.

Several things affect me. My grandfather was known to always be drunk and loud. I couldn't escape it, and it embarrassed me. I wanted to distance myself from him. My oldest uncle did the exact same thing, another had his own issues, and the list goes on and on. You were at the core of the problem, and no one ever knew, not even you. There was no father to look up to, and in my mind, I had nothing. I lacked that sense of pride to build a foundation of maturity and self-respect needed to become a man. Yes, I learned it but not from you, and you were the one I wanted to teach me those things. You should have wanted to be the one to teach me, yet here we are without any communication even now. Although I would have visits from Mom, they were just that - visits. There was always a sense of emptiness about my mother's and my relationship. Not that she didn't show affection and love because she did. I think it was equally as difficult for me to bond with her as it was for her to bond with me. I believe that her relationship with you had a lot to do with that. Because I didn't feel the love or understand who I was, the end result was resentment and pain. It's not fair to lie to your children about who they are or where they come from, or better yet say nothing at all. So instead, I painted my own picture and became a victim of the false illusion that you cared for me. Both you and Mom allowed this fantasy and the pain, because neither of you felt it important to tell me the truth.

Because of your absence and inability to do the right thing, what could have been an easy transition into becoming a man could very well have turned into a major catastrophe. I had to learn how to camouflage the pain and hurt through your absence and the secrets surrounding you. I thought it was for my good, but in reality, it was only hurting me. I guess it's safe to say that I became resistant to performing and learning in school, because I felt inferior from within. I didn't trust anyone, because I felt no one trusted me. I felt I had to lie about who I was and what I had to be in order that others accepted me. I had in a sense tried to look like a lion, but in reality was more like a curled up, shy kitten.

For some reason, Dad, I couldn't get it together. I was spiraling out of control, and I hated going to school. There was little anyone could do to change that. I was still pretending things were going well to everyone, but my life was just a plain mess. The shame of feeling "just not good enough" had taken over my thoughts. The older I got, the more resentment and anger I harbored on the inside. I was angry because of you and everyone else who participated in the cover up of your identity. I couldn't then nor do I understand now why there's a big deal of not just being honest and dealing with the truth. I covered up my pain managed briefly to keep my bad behavior and failing grades a secret. You weren't there to keep me in check, and that should have been the most important thing that a father needs to do to make his son successful.

I took advantage of the fact that my grandparents didn't have a car and weren't going to come to the school for PTA meetings or teacher conferences, keeping them out of the loop by never talking about the problems at school. Since there was no one to contradict my story, I was able to lie back at them. The way the report cards were in those days you could easily change the F to a B, which is what I did most of the time. Intellectually, it wouldn't have been hard to earn the better grade, but my stubborn side wanted no part of that. I knew no one was going to pay that much attention. Not that my family didn't care or weren't concerned, they just didn't know what to look for or see the problems. Eventually, there was no escaping the fact that I was failing, and if I didn't make some fast changes, I was certain to quit school, get kicked out, or to get so far behind I couldn't graduate at all. I was so far behind that I couldn't see any signs of graduating. I managed to alienate most of the teachers with my smart mouth and refusal to learn. I felt there was no place to turn.

There was so much to make up, so many classes I failed. I was now a year behind, and any slips would put me two years behind. It was getting to the end of the school year, and I was screwed. I knew that time was up. How was I going to cover that lie up? I became desperate and was scrambling to find a way to graduate with my class. In order to graduate, I needed to have perfect grades and go to summer school, too. I had simply wasted valuable time with reckless behavior.

Never once did I ask the guidance counselor for advice or direction nor did she offer her services. I never spoke to anyone in my family; I just kept trying to fix the mess I created alone. Each time I made one-step forward I found myself taking two-steps back. I couldn't ask for help, because I was failing and I had painted such a bright picture I was passing. By doing that, I'd backed myself into a corner with no way out. I had to do the best I could to fix it myself or continue to hide the truth and hope something magical happened. I was hard-headed, but more than that, I was scared. I was so mixed up that I didn't know what to do. On the one hand, I didn't want to disappoint my grandmother, but I was doing exactly that but couldn't ask for her help. My house of cards was about to come crashing down, and I couldn't stop the wind from blowing them to the floor. The lies were getting bigger, and I had no idea how to come clean, because it had been going on for so long.

The "Game of Pretend" that I started at an early age began to take a strong hold of me and for a long time refused to let go. I wanted to fit in and felt the only way was to create a fictional character that everyone loved or wanted to associate with. Dad, this is what I did to myself. If I felt you were getting too close or were about to see the real me, I would write you off or become a different person with a new background. I'd make up stories about you, Dad, and who you were. I had everything. I could talk about the political points on the news programs; I watched them, but I didn't apply that knowledge in class. I used it to create a new me instead. If you talk to anyone who knew me at this time, they would know me as the pretend person not the real me. I really was a confused teenager with internal secrets, looking for answers in all the wrong places.

Make no mistake. I was very proud and displayed extreme confidence on the outside. I know I had great grandparents that treated me like their youngest child not an outsider. My mother, stepfather, aunts, and uncles were as supportive as they knew to be, but they couldn't support or assist me in the things they could not see. There was always something missing. That something was you, the absent father that no one wanted to talk about, and if they did, they lied or pretended you didn't exist. Nothing was ever enough, because I really wanted to know who I was. I've always wanted more, and any accomplishments had no significance to me because of this. The more I pretended to have a father, the more inquisitive I became, and the more I rebelled, because I felt abandoned by you.

I yearned for your presence so much that, when men would come visit my aunts or if there were men that came to our home for large family occasions, it became a time to sit and imagine if they were you. Why any father would do that to a child is beyond me. How did you sleep at night being that man, Dad? You reduced me to sitting and listening for clues from other men to try and know you and find you. I studied their behavior to see if one of them could possibly be something like me and just maybe finally be you. Could this be my dad? Could he? Those were the lengths I would go to connect to you in my imagination. I would listen very carefully to see if any hints of a possible relationship with my mother would arise between these men and her, so I could end the speculation and questions. If I found a man I liked, I would say to myself, "I bet that's my dad" or "I wish he was my dad."

I would do the same thing for television characters. For instance, the show *60 minutes* had an anchor by the name of Ed Bradley. He was so cool, and I loved watching the show every Sunday evening. My mother always thought of him to be such a handsome man, so I wanted to act like him and draw from his character. I would wonder could he be my dad since my mother lived in New York, but I knew that wasn't so. I tried to pattern myself after the character of Victor Newman, because he had so much power and so many people feared and admired him. Those that crossed him he made pay, and that was very intriguing to me. The women adored his charisma and charm, so I watched the show with my aunts and tried to master his character's personality and make it part of my own. Any male I found intriguing, I tried to be them. I could just keep becoming all these men. As I write this letter to you, I am amazed that I'm actually admitting this and have the nerves to write it down. Perception and reality are miles apart. My internal pain and unwillingness to communicate were cries for help, whether you were there or not. Through this letter, Dad, I take back my life and release the pain I felt because you weren't there for me.

Looking back now, Dad, I can see some blessings in the pain. I always surround myself with people that don't bore me. I surround myself with creative thinkers, dreamers of possibilities, and those with everyday common sense. I was always thinking. I knew from the slides shown to me in Ms. Walkers' class that there was more out there beyond McBee, and I was going to find it with or without you. I was just that determined, but I was going about it the wrong way.

Had I applied half of my intellect and creative thoughts to school and not to an *invisible* father I could have been more than a model student.

I had then and possess now the power to be whatever I want to be. After years of searching, wondering, and pretending I now realize I am who I am. Though you made me, I won't allow your absence to break me. This is a road to internal healing and self-discovery, so I can be a better me and be a better father. It is through this letter that I can forgive the *invisible* you.

Anthony

DAD, I WISH YOU HAD MET MS. BOLTZ, THE HIGH SCHOOL TEACHER RESPONSIBLE FOR SAVING ME FROM MYSELF.

JUST WHEN I THOUGHT NO ONE cared and things were nearing the breaking point, I found hope in a special teacher that I really liked and began to connect with her. I still had moments of defiance in class, but she had a certain persuasion. By all accounts, this is my absolute favorite high school teacher. A very witty woman, she made it clear she was not amused by my silly antics. My life in high school really started to change as she began to give meaning to my life. This is the one teacher who broke the code and peeled back the fake surface I was showing everyone. Ms. Boltz was the most magnificent woman at McBee High. For no reason, I was failing English, a subject that I knew very well. I lived in detention for being nothing more than an arrogant, outspoken, lazy student, yet she still saw my potential. Nothing I tried could fool her. She saw right through me and began to work with me and challenge me. She knew I was not as dumb as I was acting. On one occasion, she sat me down after class and tells me that I was playing a game that I was not going to win. She began to probe and ask me questions to find out why I had so much anger and resentment towards everyone. She was the first person to ever ask me those things. Through our many conversations, I could see she knew more about me than I knew about myself. I found myself captivated by her tough side.

She balanced discipline with displays of genuine concern and an eagerness to try and build on the qualities that I managed to hide inside.

Despite our relationship, I still had my moments of being disrespectful in her class. Finally, one day after pushing the envelope too far, Ms. Boltz had finally had enough. I was told to come back to her class at the end of the day or face detention once again. When I returned to her room at the end of the day, I found myself faced with her life-changing ultimatum. She looked at me in utter frustration, and I could tell that I was not in a position to act silly or belligerent anymore. She told me she had a plan, and I had no option but to follow it. She reached into her desk and pulled out two things: a detention slip for three days and a 4-H essay/public speaking entry form. This was my choice: take the three days detention or write the essay to compete in the contest. Normally, I would have just taken the detention, but I couldn't do that this time, because I already had 12 days of detention on the book, and 3 more would give me 15, resulting in a three-day suspension. As much as I would have liked to have the days off from school, my grandmother would have literally flipped. Not to mention, she would have to come to the school, and my cover would be blown. My grandmother would find out that I wasn't doing well in school, I was going to fail that grade, and how many days I had been in in-school suspension. I had so many secrets to keep. This was definitely motivation to do the essay instead. I tried to talk Mrs. Boltz out of the contest part, but nothing I said worked. I was not interested in writing essays or public speaking, but her mind was made up. She refused to listen to my pleas any longer. She stood up from her desk and said, "Well, Anthony, you have three days detention for being silly and hardheaded. Maybe when you come back to school, you will want to do something with your life. Now get out of my class. I'm done talking. You've wasted enough of my time." Realizing I had run out of excuses and options, I said: "Wait, I will do the essay." She had my attention. No one had ever succeeded at doing that before. I had three days to write the essay and have it back to her or the three days detention that I didn't choose would become five days instead. There was no escaping the suspension if I didn't follow through. She knew how to be an enforcer, but essentially she was handing me a future and finding a passion for something I didn't know I had.

As I left her classroom feeling defeated with those entry forms and guidelines in my hand, I had no idea what I was doing. I rarely did my homework, so following through on this was certainly going to be a challenge. After reading the forms, I realized how much time this was going to take and the hours I would have to spend in the library doing research on the subject. For me, going to the library was rare, especially since studying was not something that interested me. My essay's subject was: "Why is water conservation important?" I didn't care about this; we were on a well. Why did I care? As I began to write and do the research, however, I became interested in the subject and started to have fun. On the third day, I turned in the completed entry form and the written essay to Ms. Boltz and took my seat in her class. She reviewed it, called me up to her desk, and asked me a simple question, "Why can't you apply this same quality to your class work? This is outstanding, Anthony." I had no answer. She went on to say, "This is proof you can do the work if you would only try. You should have better grades than you do so I'm going to see how we can make this work for you. I'm going to enter this in the county 4-H contest with Mr. Sweeney, the man in charge of the 4-H activities for the county. I believe you have a great chance in winning the county one and possibly even state." I was shocked and somewhat excited until she said: "Now, I have to prepare you to speak in public." I said to her in frustration and anger: "That's not part of the deal. I'm not interested in speaking like that. I'm only writing the essay to stay out of trouble." I was not given any options, and the only thing she said to me was "Get to it."

Although I read the minutes in Sunday school as the secretary, public speaking was unfamiliar territory for me. Speaking intelligently to an audience of classmates that normally saw me as the troublemaker and class instigator was not an image I wanted. I wasn't interested in losing that image of "cool", but fortunately, I wasn't in charge, because that image was getting me nowhere fast. In the weeks that lead up to the contest, Ms. Boltz arranged for me to visit various classes and practice my speech. In return, the class would critique me, ask questions, and give feedback. For the most part, the other teachers and my fellow students were amazed at my speaking abilities. No one was used to seeing that side of me, and I liked the feeling of confidence. The ultimatum was now going to either result in victory, which was a long shot, or end in embarrassment.

When the time came, Mr. Sweeny arrived to the school for his monthly 4-H meeting with students in the cafeteria. Ms. Boltz and I arrived with the entry form. He reviewed it and made me give the speech again to the 4-H group. This was the first time he ever heard me speak other than being a loud mouth during his meetings. After I was done, he gave me a pat on the back and said; "I think if you do that in Chesterfield County next week you will be declared the winner." I wasn't really confident he was right. The only thing I could think of was going against really smart students who had been applying themselves much better than I had been doing recently.

The day of the contest, Mr. Sweeney came to the school to give me a ride to Chesterfield. As he drove, I practiced my speech and talked to him about the competition. I wanted to know as much as I could since I had never entered this kind of competition. Upon our arrival at the 4-H extension office, I joined the other contestants seated in the hall. Everyone was nervous as we prepared ourselves to stand and speak before a panel of three judges, some parents, and a group of staff. I didn't have anyone there with me for support during the competition. When my name was called, I went to the podium with my notecards. We weren't allowed to bring the actual written speech. We had to memorize it. I gave my speech and when finished thanked the judges. As I stepped down, I looked closely at the judges, but they gave no indication of how they viewed my delivery or the quality of the speech. When everyone was done, they called us back into the room. They congratulated each of us for our efforts and then proceeded with the awards ceremony. They started with third place and worked their way up. Not hearing my name for third or second, I was nervous. I knew all of the contestants were good but wasn't sure I had given a winning speech. When the announcer said the winner was Anthony Outen from McBee High School, I couldn't believe it. I must have heard them wrong, but I had actually won the contest that I didn't want to enter and had beaten students with far better grades. No one had a clue that I was failing all my classes or was so far behind back at my high school. I received a check for $25.00, had my picture taken for the newspaper, and went back to McBee triumphant.

The next day when I returned to school, my first stop was Ms. Boltz's class. She was so excited for me, and it was nice to hear my name over the morning speaker as the winner of the public speaking contest. Now, I had some serious thinking to do about the way I was performing in school. For the first time in my life, I felt like a winner. I didn't have to pretend to win; I actually did it and wanted more.

Ms. Boltz continued to enter me into contests and encouraged me to stay motivated. I competed and won them all. No matter how good I was at winning speaking awards, that alone was not going to help me graduate. Mrs. Boltz would often tell me, "Pull your head out of your rear, and stop letting excuses control your life. Accept responsibility for what you have done. Stop failing and move forward." She was more than a teacher; she was saving me from myself. We both knew I was so far behind in my grades that passing that year was nearly impossible, but she kept pushing me. Everyone else had given up, even me, but she was not interested in my plans to quit school. I wanted nothing to do with school because I thought I couldn't graduate and was not interested in hearing what anyone had to say on the subject. All I could think about was my friends preparing to graduate at the end of that year, and I was stuck. Yes, it was of my own doing but that didn't make the pain any easier to bear. I felt as though nothing mattered, but true to her character, persuasive Ms. Boltz always gets her way. She knew I was seriously considering not returning to school, so she pushed for me to enter the ultimate contest in public speaking, the national contest. If I won this one, she said, it could change everything. This contest came with more exposure and could lead to more than local or state notoriety. It had national recognition, and this was important to me. However, in order for me to enter, I had to remain a student and return to school next year to graduate. On top of that, I had less than two weeks to fill out the entry form and prepare the essay.

I was so angry at the time I didn't even want to look at any teacher or my schoolmates for that matter. I told Mrs. Boltz I didn't think I had it in me, that too much had happened. I didn't want to go down as a loser in public speaking, too. She said, "Anthony, you lose if you walk away and quit school. Do that and all you have won so far will mean nothing if you quit now. How do you think it will look for the number one speaker in this school and all over the state to quit and not graduate? That's down right stupid. Now, get over it! What are you thinking? You know you don't want to do that. That's the easy way out, and you will always regret it." She began to turn red, and I knew she was getting mad, so I quickly changed my attitude. After all, I knew she was right. Then she made me count to twelve forward. I thought she was crazy, but I did it. Then she made me count to twelve backwards, and I did it. When I was done, she explained, "Now when you feel like giving up, count to twelve forwards and then backwards. That's the numbers of months you have left including summer before you will graduate. Before you know it, Anthony, your time here will be done, but the choice is yours. The time goes fast. You failed to apply yourself and do your best over the years, and it has brought you to this point. You chose this path. Now, walk it to the end. Since you're not going to graduate this year, do something positive with your time and leave here a winner. Don't worry about those other boys graduating; focus on when you will leave." I was still not convinced. If I lost, then that would be the last thought anyone would have of me. She then looked at me as she put the form in my hand and said; "Well, Anthony, I guess you better not lose. Now, get to it."

Reluctantly, I agreed to do it as if I had a real choice. It's true I needed something to motivate me and offer balance. Without something to keep me focused, I would certainly collapse. Out of respect and appreciation for her, I was determined to make her proud. She stuck with me from the beginning, and this was the least I could do to repay her and help myself in the process. If I pulled it off, I would compete in Washington, DC. This would be my most challenging essay, and it came at a time when I was at my weakest point. The entry had multiple levels of competition making it more complex in presentation and more competitive. One major win could actually result in three minor wins and would mean multiple speaking engagements to represent South Carolina on a national scale.

This new essay was so much harder than the rest, and I worked long past midnight, striving for perfection. My grandmother was now aware that I would have to go one more year to high school was still quite upset at me for failing in school. She would sit quietly in her chair the entire time I was writing. She didn't go to bed until I was done, and never said anything. She just continued to read her *Bible* and her faith magazine to pass time. I think she was sitting there praying for a miracle, because that's what it would take to get me straight, keep me motivated, and for me to finally graduate from high school.

After days of research and writing, I was finished. I took the essay and the necessary forms to Ms. Boltz for her approval. She had me make some minor changes, but it passed. Relieved to have completed my last contest entry, I took the packet to the post office at once feeling confident and uncertain. I had never lost before, but the possibility of humiliation and additional stress was taking a serious toll on me.

Weeks later, near the end of the school year, there was a letter from the sponsors of the contest. It was a thick envelope that could only mean one thing that I had won a spot in the contest, but I wasn't sure. I opened the letter, and sure enough, I was chosen as one of 15 from the entire state of South Carolina to go to Washington, DC. I won part one of the competition I didn't want to enter, at the absolute lowest time in my life. Part one was over, but I was about to compete again for the biggest competition of my life. I accepted defeat from failing and not graduating and turned it into a bigger victory through not giving up. Once again, Ms. Boltz saw something in me that I didn't see in myself.

In the back of my mind, when she said this contest had national recognition, I thought if I get national recognition, then you have to see me, Dad. You aren't going to be able to ignore me or pretend that I don't exist anymore. This was my chance for me to let you know that I'm doing good. Winning this contest was more for you to see me than for me to win this contest to graduate high school or help my future. I was winning and it became more opportunities for me to get your attention. I was still doing stupid stuff, but I was trying to get you to notice me. I wanted you to say "You know, that's my son," if you saw my picture. I wanted you to be bragging to your friends, "That's my son. He's doing pretty good down there in South Carolina." But again, it wasn't going to happen.

Anthony

DAD, I DIDN'T PLAY SPORTS, BUT I WAS INFLUENCED BY TWO GREAT COACHES.

THE SCHOOL FOOTBALL COACH WAS COACH Roberts, my friend and mentor, though he may not have known it. I tried out, but I couldn't play football. I only made it through the first practice. I wasn't big on getting hit and sweating. I tried out but couldn't play basketball, so what could build a bond between a coach and a guy with virtually no athletic abilities? As with everything else, help usually comes from the unexpected and when you're least expecting it. One day, Coach Roberts just started talking to me, and to this day, I don't know why, but I am thankful that he did. It was nice to have someone take an interest in me. Our relationship had nothing to do with sports. He was my driver's education teacher, but other than that, we had little contact. His class was one of the very few classes that kept my attention, and I didn't have any issues or confrontations. He seemed to be a genuine man that almost everyone liked and respected. Both the basketball and football teams won countless district and state championships with him as coach, so his popularity was obvious. He was a proven winner, and I always liked surrounding myself with winners.

His car, an old gray and burgundy station wagon, was absolutely the dirtiest car I had ever seen. He often carried athletes around in it, and he had very young children so that didn't help matters. During driver's education class, he overheard me talking about my job helping my uncle Bo detail cars. When the bell rang, he asked me did I have plans on Saturday.

I said no, and he invited me over. If I had known he wanted me to help him clean his car from the start, I may not have given that answer. I knew what that car looked like, and it was going to take a miracle to get it clean. Today, asking me over to clean a car doesn't sound like much, and to some may seem insulting; however, in those days you were glad to do anything for honest money. At least that was the case for me. Besides that I was talking about an invitation to Coach Roberts' house, and I was always in search for acceptance and recognition of other men since you weren't around.

Sometimes, I wondered why he took an interest in me. I wasn't an athlete. I just thought: "What the heck?" and it was something to do with someone different. I arrived at his house that Saturday morning expecting to be left alone outside to clean his car, get paid, and be on my way. I knocked on the door to find things would be quite the opposite, because Coach Roberts opened the door and invited me in. The family was sitting down to breakfast and wanted me to join them. I was hesitant. I'm a very picky eater, but he wouldn't take no for an answer. My grandmother always told me it was more polite to say no to this kind of offer in case they really couldn't afford to share their food. Just like she said not to go over someone's house at dinner time unless you were invited. You should have eaten before you got there to be polite. So, I was reluctant, but I decided to join them and enjoyed the cordial conversations.

After eating breakfast, we both proceeded outside to wash the car. He helped me the entire time. He said, "You didn't think I was going to make you clean this dirty car all by yourself, did you?" I thought to myself, "Well actually, yes, I did." We talked a lot and enjoyed a few laughs. Never once did he mention school or why I had to do the things I did to get into trouble. I viewed him in a different light from then on. He didn't treat me the way I had expected him to. I was anticipating questions and counseling about my bad behavior and poor grades. After all, he was a teacher. I was prepared to be defensive, but there was no need. I was feeling substandard, and my self-esteem was low. I was not raised to feel inferior to anyone, but often felt that way. Thinking back now, I felt that way, because I had degraded myself by my actions. I had feelings of guilt because of my selfish behavior for years. When you know you're better than you act or perform, there is always resentment from within yourself. I had never been afraid of hard work; I was used to that from being in the peach fields. I have always been taught that honorable work has its place. The job you hate the most will often lead you to a better job with more rewards. I've always lived by that philosophy, and it's true. Tough things build character, and character is sought after more than any other quality.

At the end of the day, Coach Roberts was as wet, sweaty, and dirty as I was. That taught me something. Never ask someone to do something you wouldn't do yourself. If it's good enough for them to do, then it's good enough for you. When we were done, the car looked amazingly clean, smelled fresh, and we both gleamed with pride. So now came the big question "Anthony, how much do I owe you?" I had no idea. Originally, I thought $20.00 but didn't expect him to help clean the car with me. Throw in the fact that by now I had eaten two meals and drank countless drinks, I was at a loss for what to charge.

Instead of giving him a price, I simply said, "Give me whatever you think its worth since you helped the whole time." He continued to press me for a price, and honestly, he had no idea that he had already paid me. He had given me Time. To me, that was worth much more than money. Money can do many things, but the one thing it doesn't do is teach life lessons and offer words of wisdom. Since I wouldn't give him a price, he simply reached into his pocket and handed me $40.00. I will never forget that. I was blown away that he paid me double what I was even thinking of asking for. He said, "Anthony, that was a dirty car, wasn't it? Thanks for helping me out." He told me that I was always welcome at his home, and if I decided I wanted to talk about anything, just to stop by. That meant a lot to me. It had nothing to do with the dirty car or the money. Coach Roberts allowed me to be me, and in his own way found a way to teach your son some important life lessons off the football field and off the basketball court. He taught me to play a different game: the game of life. Perhaps, he felt I needed to talk to someone, but instead of forcing the issue, he simply extended an invitation and offered his time. When you know that someone cares, you begin to care.

Another coach, Coach Gaskins, taught me things even he didn't imagine he would. To say the least, there was a time that I didn't like him at all, and I'm sure the feelings were mutual. He was stigmatized as a racist by some of the guys I associated with. I stayed away from him and gave him nasty looks when I would see him in the hall. A strict disciplinarian, he gave some of the hardest licks, the harshest punishment for bad behavior, than anyone at the school. In my opinion, he just looked plain mean and hateful.

As time went on, I realized that the label the other boys had given him was not true. I was no stranger to Coach Gaskins' office. I was always in trouble for one thing or the other. Though I had these preconceptions of him, he did not judge me quite as harshly, though he very well could have. After all, I hadn't set the bar very high with the record I had in school. In those days, students were allowed to drive a school bus if you could pass the rigorous written and practical driving tests. However, before you could do any of that, you had to first convince Coach Gaskins, the one in charge of the school bus driver assignments, that you could handle the responsibility of driving a school bus. You had to prove you were dependable, disciplined, and responsible. I didn't have a lot going for me and meeting this criterion was about as far from reality as me being a star athlete.

But I wanted to be a driver really bad and decided to ask for a meeting with Coach Gaskins to plead my case. Without hesitation, he abruptly told me No! He actually asked me was I joking, because I couldn't possibly be serious. Well, as devastating as that was to hear, he went on to tell me why. He named just a few reasons. "You're hardheaded. You're always in trouble. You don't listen. You can't seem to stay out of detention, so why on earth should I trust you to drive my school bus loaded with children? We haven't even discussed your grades, and they aren't even good enough." I sat in complete silence. Then he said something I heard as a challenge. "Besides all of that, Anthony, I don't even think you're smart enough to pass the written test." Had he not said that, I would have simply turned and walked away, because he was right about the things he had said. I couldn't argue those facts. I had no defense. But when he said the word *can't*, that word spoke to me. My grandmother always told me to never accept *can't* as your reality, or you will never be anything. He had challenged me, and I loved a good challenge then and still do today. Never tell me that I can't do something.

Finally, I knew I had better speak fast and be very persuasive. I didn't deny the things he said as not true because they were. I did have some nerve walking into his office thinking I had a chance to drive a school bus. He was right, but my brain went into overdrive quickly realizing I would lose the debate unless I spoke up. The only thing I could do was say, "I know I can pass the test, and I will prove you wrong if you give me a chance. I will also prove to you that I can do better in every class and with my behavior. Give me a chance to prove you wrong, and I will become a better student and change the things I've been doing immediately." That's it; that's all I had. He looked at me with a piercing stare, leaned back in his chair, for what felt like hours gave me no facial expression or emotion. I was thinking either my declaration was going to fly or it wasn't. Finally, he relented, "Ok, Anthony. Here's what I'm going to do. I will allow you to sit for the bus driving class and take the written test. If you pass, which I personally don't think will happen, and if you do anything that pisses me off, I will make sure you never drive a bus. Is that understood?" "Yes sir," I replied, and with that, the meeting was over, and I had some major changes to make.

Soon, it was time for the driving classes to begin, and I sat for the required instruction to prepare for the written test. Occasionally, Coach Gaskins would pop his head in the door, point at me glaring with that mean stare, and leave. I will never forget that. Now, looking back, I believe he was pulling for me and that was his way to show support, though that wasn't my view at the time. Often the people we think want us to fail are the very ones pushing for us to succeed. Soon, it was test time, and I was praying to pass. I took my time, checking and double checking every answer. The test was hard, but I was confident enough to turn it in early. As I sat quietly watching the instructor grade it, I felt so much stress. I wanted to pass and be able to have my bus license, but I also wanted to prove Coach Gaskins wrong equally as much. After the grading was done, the next words the instructor spoke were a bit unnerving. Unfortunately, everyone didn't pass. My heart started racing. He began to call our names, and we went up to the desk for the results of our exams. When my name was called, I didn't look at my test until I sat back down. I had passed, and better than just pass, I had only missed three questions, another major accomplishment. Who knew; why couldn't I apply that same resilience to the subjects that mattered so that I could pass other classes in school? I remember actually asking myself that question while sitting there staring at my test. For some reason, it did not register why I couldn't apply that same energy to the other classes. I did everything I wanted to do with great accomplishment, but did nothing that I needed to do to accomplish the things that really mattered. With the results in hand, I went running to prove my point to Coach Gaskins. When I arrived, I said, "I told you I was going to pass." Expecting congratulations, I simply got, "Well, so what. You don't have a license yet. That test proves nothing. Are you passing any other classes yet?" I thought: What is wrong with this man? Who does he think he is? But he was simply doing his job, because I was still far from completing the challenge.

Some weeks later, we were loaded on busses with instructors to begin our road training. It seemed as if the training classes were going to take forever. I had driven a little with Mr. Lester, and my uncles had let me drive a few times here and there, but with no car came very little driving experience. I was nervous, because I wasn't very familiar with a stick shift, and the bus was huge and intimidating. Not only did I have to drive, but at the same time I had to explain everything I was doing. If that wasn't enough, I also had to prove to Coach Gaskins that I was not going to fail this test. I was determined to not give him the satisfaction of saying "I told you so".

When it was my turn, I did great. I passed the test. I was issued a school bus driver's license and was eligible to have a driving route. With a smile and a sense of victory, once again I ran off to see Coach Gaskins. I had proven him wrong and wanted to see what he had to say this time. "Anthony, although I'm impressed that you have passed and have your license, I never promised you anything. I only agreed to let you take the test, and see if you could pass. I've done all I said I would do. Now, if you want to drive, you have to prove to me that I should trust you to drive." Quietly thinking to myself, I was getting rather angry. What? More conditions, you have got to be kidding me. What seemed like victory turned out to be only a half-time lead. I couldn't get into any trouble, couldn't get kicked out of class, had to get my grades up, and the list went on and on. To meet his standard was actually going to be harder than getting the license itself. I had to change my image and reputation of being a silly, nonproductive fool and become a disciplined and focused young man. I wasn't going to get any breaks from him unless I gave that bad boy image up.

That was the challenge. I'm not saying that I became the model student, but it was another defining moment, leading me in the right direction. I was being forced to grow up, and it was hard. I had mastered the public speaking stage, the drum, and my bus driver's license. It was now time to focus on things that would actually contribute to getting me out of school and being taken seriously. I met none of the criteria, yet the trust Coach Gaskins gave me to even try was more than I had given myself. My intentional failing to even try in the important things could have very well resulted in my failure in life goals. As time passed, I demonstrated behavior fitting of a responsible bus driver, I was added to the roster as just a substitute driver. My grades improved, I drove often, and I earned money and a sense of pride.

After doing so well, naturally, I had to do something to mess it all up. I got kicked out of class again for doing something stupid. I'm not sure exactly what I was arguing, but I remember the consequences. Just as I was in the middle of talking back to my teacher, in walks Coach Gaskins as if he was psychic and knew I was doing something wrong. Oh God, what have I done now? He pulled me out of the class and into the hall. I tried to plead my case, but the damage was done. I argued, "She can't do anything to me. She doesn't know what she's talking about. She can't tell me what to do. I didn't do nothing wrong." He simply responded, "Maybe she can't hurt you, but I can. Give me your license!" I looked at him in shock, but he continued, "Don't make me ask you again. I said give me your license now, Anthony!" I had no choice; I handed the license to him, but he wasn't finished with me. "You lose. Now, Loser, get back into the classroom and keep your mouth shut." Once again, I let my mouth and my inability to just sit down, be quiet, and do my class work cause me to look like a complete fool. Embarrassed, I walked back into the class, although pretending nothing happened, sat down and said nothing. I could have done that before not argued with my teacher, but I guess that made too much sense. Now, I had no bus license after all that work. I remained angry at Coach Gaskins, but I knew I had done it to myself. Even so, I did my best to avoid him at all costs. I was more embarrassed than anything, because I realized I lost because of me not because of his discipline of my bad behavior.

Months would pass, and one day, Mr. Gaskins stopped me in the hall. He said, "I heard from Coach Roberts you liked cleaning cars, and you do a very good job. Do you mind helping me out after school?" Really, I thought to myself, help you? Nevertheless, I met him out front at his car after school. I didn't have much to say to him as we left for his house. It was a strange ride. I was riding with this man who took my bus license from me, and I was still not very happy about it. When we arrived, he invited me into his house, told me what he wanted done, and then simply gave me the keys to the car. "Bring it back when you're done." I was shocked. You mean Coach Gaskins trusts me with his car after all the history and things I had done wrong at school? He didn't give me any set time to return just money to buy the things I needed to clean the car. It became like a boasting thing. I had to make sure I was seen in the car. No one would ever believe he gave me the keys to his Regal unless they saw me driving it. So, I cleaned the car and returned it that evening. He paid me well and thanked me for doing a good job. Giving me a ride back into town, he said nothing about my confiscated bus license nor did I. He didn't bring up school or my behavior, quite identical to the way Coach Roberts had treated me.

Weeks went by, and one day he came by one of my classes to see me. Immediately, I began to think negatively, because the last time we were in the hall it wasn't a pretty picture, because I had obviously done something wrong again. This time, he asked me if I had learned my lesson, did I know how to act. I said I had and I did. He reached into his wallet, pulled out my license, and gave it back to me. I stared at it since I didn't know he still had it, because normal procedure was to send it back to the county office. "By the way, Anthony, you're driving today. I have a route for you, and don't mess this up." I was elated to say the least, but true to my form, I displayed no emotion, keeping it cool. From that day on, I never lost my right to drive buses, and he kept me busy as a cover driver. Although he had quite a different approach than Coach Roberts, this man broke me down and built me back up in a different kind of way that gave me an appreciation of respect and accountability. Trust and accountability builds character.

Coach Gaskins gave me a choice to do right or wrong. He made me test my own character. He made me work for what I wanted rather than giving me a free ride with my excuses. Doing the right thing wasn't hard; I just made doing the wrong thing look too easy. I also learned to never judge someone based on the words of others. If my mind would have remained closed, Dad, I could have never reached my potential. I had to learn not to only associate with people that look and think like me. When my courage and strength allowed me to look further than the things I didn't have, I began to see the many blessing I have without you. The accountability and discipline are the common factors that bring your hopes and dreams to reality. These men taught me that, and maybe if you read this letter, you will find these life lessons as well.

Your Son,

Anthony

DAD, I STARTED GAINING NATIONAL RECOGNITION. DID YOU SEE ME?

BEING THE FIRST AFRICAN-AMERICAN FROM OUR school to win a public speaking award on a national level came with much recognition and accolades throughout my community. Although the main expenses of the trip to the second stage of the competition, meals and hotel accommodations, were paid fully by the contest sponsor, I had no wardrobe to meet the senators and house members on the itinerary in Washington, DC, where it would take place. Additionally, there was a visit to the White House for a South Lawn presentation for those who made it to the second stage. I only had one suit, a few dress shirts, and maybe a couple pairs of slacks. Once my winning essays began to appear in the newspapers, the phone started ringing with offers of support. Bishop James of the Living Church in the Lord Jesus Christ was so inspired that he paid me a visit. His church made a generous donation to me and that meant so much for travelling to these contests and for other expenses. He gave me great support even though I wasn't a member of his church. My home church, Shady Grove Missionary Baptist Church, also gave me a generous donation during Sunday morning worship. The entire community rallied behind me during this time, and this motivated me to want to make a change for the better and move past the pain I felt because of my lack of a connection with you.

One day my grandfather came home from working in the yard of a prominent older white lady in town. Mrs. King had shown him a newspaper clipping of me winning the first stage of a major public speaking competition, wanting to know if my grandfather knew this Anthony Outen. He told her I was his grandson. "She was very proud of you," he told me. As weeks went by, Ms. King called my grandmother and requested I come by her house after school. I can still remember seeing her, a pale, elderly lady with long grayish-blue hair that blew in the wind as she sat talking to me in her backyard. She thought it was wonderful to see a young man from McBee representing the state. I stood beside her patiently listening, wondering why she cared so much. It was interesting to be in that moment. Here I was the grandson of her groundskeeper and she was congratulating me for winning and going to the nation's capital. All the while, my grandfather was working, sweating as he cleaned the brush and hedges around her backyard. "I have something for you." She pointed to her old brown station wagon parked near the shed and told me to look in the backseat. In that backseat were nice suit bags from Belk's and BC Moores with enough clothes to cover most of the week for my Washington trip. We didn't shop there very often because the prices were higher than we could afford. She opened the bags and showed me what she had purchased and said she hoped the salesperson picked things I liked. My grandmother must have given her my sizes. I was very excited but again was not one to show a lot of emotion. There were suits, slacks, shirts, and ties to match. She then reached beside her seat cushion and handed me a check made payable to my grandmother for $100.00. She instructed me to give it directly to her and said this is for anything else you may need and for spending money. "Go and do well and make us proud." While my grandfather continued to trim hedges, never pausing in his work, I thanked her for her generosity. Looking back now, I think about how for years he labored on her farm for mere pennies per hour and shelter for his family; however, on that day he had the opportunity to see all of his labor was not in vain. As history shows he was clearing the path for me. Proof that the reward may not come to you, but there will be blessings for future generations that will benefit from the labor you endure.

While in Washington, I won the second stage of the competition. I defeated the 14 students from our district and over 30 from across the state. I became the student that would represent South Carolina to compete against the other 49 states. This winning on a national level came with the opportunity to meet many powerful people in Washington, DC.

I was now moving to the third and final stage of the competition. I flew back to South Carolina with yet another win under my belt, and a renewal of pride. There was no time to play around because the final stage of national competitions would begin in a few months in New Orleans.

It was necessary to stay in school one more year and try and graduate, an uphill battle. It was still going to be a struggle to make it through this tough year. Because of my poor performance of previous years, I had a lot of work to do, and I had to pass every single class in order to graduate. I had accomplished much out of the classroom; I now had to find the motivation to put as much effort into school as I did public speaking. I knew I had it in me, but for some reason I was fighting against myself. I desperately wanted to bring the dream to a reality, but I was not going to be an "A" student. Everyone is not meant to be that. I could, however, be the best I could be instead of just getting by or failing altogether. Unfortunately, that's' easier said than done. Some weeks I did well, and then some I didn't do anything. Although I was well aware of the consequences, I wavered in sound judgment. School was not the same for me, but I was making the best of it.

Going to New Orleans to speak at the national convention of the NREA's annual meeting was truly a big deal, the third stage of the national competition. Few could say they had ever gone this far, and I did it with the absolute worst grades and under unbelievable circumstances. From my successful public speaking, I was getting used to eating in five-star restaurants. Even though, I had no idea what the stars meant. Coming from a small town, plates weren't presented like portraits in a magazine. I had been taught by Mr. Sweeny, my 4-H mentor, how to use proper etiquette in these situations. I was used to eating the entire meal with the same fork. I won the competition at the Superdome. There were so many people there that I almost panicked. I stood in victory and pride, representing the state of South Carolina. Of the 50 students, there were only 4 African-Americans, and I won. I had exceeded not only my expectations but those of everyone who knew me. I didn't appreciate until later the gravity of what I had done.

After winning numerous smaller competitions across the state and across the country and even winning the national award over 50 other young people, my family finally heard me speak for the first time in competition. I always had wanted the support of family in the audience, but I had not had it before. The SEC was very proud of my winning the second stage in Washington, DC, and had invited me to speak at their annual meeting. This event would be the first time Grandma and Mom would see me on stage. They had seen me do things in church but not in the public speaking capacity with the reaction of such a large audience. Until that moment, they only read about me, and I don't think either of them truly realized what I had accomplished in spite of my other failures. One thing I always wanted was for my family to see me do something that I liked to do, and see what I had accomplished. I don't think they understood what it meant to me to have them there and be a part of what I was doing.

When we arrived and my grandmother saw all of the cars at the event, she said: "What are all these people doing here? Are you usually talking to this many people?" I smiled, "Sometimes, but I think this is a lot more than usual for an event in South Carolina." My speech was short, but the introduction onto the stage was as big as it gets. The little boy that could was about to step in front of over 2000 people and my family. As I gave my speech about winning in the public speaking contests, they cheered as if I had won the Superbowl. As I stood on stage looking at so many people cheering for me, it was my Superbowl moment. I could see my grandmother and my mother down front in a sea of people beaming with pride. It would have been nice to have shared that moment with you also, Dad. At least for that brief moment, I felt I had made up for failing and not doing my best in school. I exited the stage feeling good. I proved that I was not a loser, and that I was somebody to more than just a few family and friends. I was still suffering and confused, battling *invisible pain* from an absent father. Though they had no idea what I was going through. I had no clue how to communicate my problems. But as with everything else, somehow I managed through the grace of God to shine in the midst of the storm that continued to rage inside of me.

I was gaining confidence in myself as others revealed their confidence and pride in me. I didn't have to continue my past behavior of acting out but could strive for success in this arena. I was smart but acting dumb. I should have been and could have been a better student but refused to apply myself. How could anyone think otherwise when you look at the picture

I painted? No one would ever expect a failing student to win countless public speaking awards. It's not typical that a failing student would even compete at the levels I did, let alone win. Well, that's exactly what was happening again and again. No one could see the internal *invisible pain* I continued to harbor within me.

Winning in my mind's twisted way of thinking gave me power. I knew that if I did my work and followed the rules, I would be like everyone else, and I didn't want to do that. It simply wasn't me, and it wasn't what I wanted to do. No one really expected me to win, so I always liked proving them wrong. I loved the look on their faces when I was repeatedly announced the winner. How did he do that? I was getting paid to talk, write, and speak but the punishments of not having self-esteem continued to be even greater. Though I didn't care that I couldn't play sports like most of my friends, I often marveled quietly at the applause they received from the crowds at the games. I wanted some of that, and now I was receiving it on a different playing field. I couldn't achieve what they did in sports, and they couldn't achieve what I was doing in public speaking. The money and local fame fascinated me. The more money the competition offered as a reward, the better I would perform. I spent more time perfecting my craft as a speaker than I did doing homework and studying for class, threatening graduating on time. Winning became an addiction. I was everywhere. I was winning against all odds, yet I was still feeling inferior and empty inside. It was never good enough. There was always something missing. Dad, you had never seen me win any of those contests, so on one hand victory felt pointless. I thought surely if I was in enough newspapers, had this much recognition, that maybe it would get your attention wherever you were. I took this silence as a continuation of your rejection of me I had somehow made my public speaking more about getting your attention than bettering myself. In a sense, I guess you could say I was winning for you, and not for me, though I had no clue where you were. I felt you knew me and everything I did, yet refused to congratulate me. This, Dad, were the lengths I went to prove to you that I was worthy of your love and attention. I wonder if you ever felt the same rejection from your father, and perhaps that's why you have chosen to pretend you didn't have a son. Yes, it would have been nice for you to have been a part of those moments, but in the end, I was still victorious even if I harbored *invisible pain*.

The countless public speaking awards I won over the years sometimes had no real meaning to me. The room was always filled with other parents that watched their children with pride, even though I was always defeating them. There were many times when the photographers wanted to take pictures of my winning moment with my family, but it was always just me by myself. My family read about my victories in the newspapers, just like everyone else who read the paper for news. I became at times immune to feeling I was completely on my own at these events. That's where I was mentally and emotionally. Winning became to mean nothing. Just like acquiring great things means nothing without the love and support of your family. There is a better reward in winning with support, but there is equal reward to lose and be hugged and told by family, "You will get it next time."

Though I continued to receive invitations to speak at various functions throughout the state, it felt empty. I was a success everywhere but where it counted: the classroom. How simple would it have been for me to do what I needed to do? Unfortunately, it took years to finally understand what I was doing to myself. The respect I thought I had gained was nothing compared to what I could have had if I was the student I pretended to be. I was proud of my accomplishments, but hating who I was. I still was suffering from major stress and feeling abandoned. I was indeed suffering from *Invisible Pain*. The support I had wasn't the support I wanted. I yearned for identity, my identity, and for you, the father I never knew.

Sincerely,

Anthony

DAD, MY MENTORING MOMENTS WITH MR. LESTER WILL BE CHERISHED FOREVER.

THE WORD "MENTOR" WASN'T USED IN those days, because everyone really took ownership in the lives of kids. If he were alive today, I would say that Mr. Lester was my mentor, but back then he was simply a friend even though our ages were more than 50 years apart. When I knew him, all of his children were grown and moved away. For at least nine months out of the year, he and Ms. Katie were empty-nesters. For the three months of summer, their house would be filled with grandchildren. He took a sincere interest in me for some reason, and I'm glad he did. It just seemed a natural bond that to this day I would consider indescribable.

The more I rebelled, the more Mr. Lester and I began to spend time together. I'm not sure if my grandmother asked him or if he just took it upon himself, but that's the way things played out. Although he was retired, he was often called upon for various odd jobs around town and in Hartsville. He taught me how to do various landscaping chores, which gave me the chance to earn extra money. Ms. Katie also allowed me to gather eggs from her chicken coop, and for my pay, I would get to keep an egg or two depending on how many were laid that day. The first time I ever drove a car was his white Plymouth Fury III two-door coupe. I wasn't old enough to drive legally, but there were plenty of country roads around for me to practice. Our town only had one police officer, and he never patrolled outside of the town limits. In a sense, I guess you could say that he played an instrumental role in keeping me out of a lot of trouble. He was also the man that had the heart to do what you didn't: Take a little time with your son to teach him some important things about becoming a man. Although I still was quite mischievous when away from him, the more time I spent time with Mr. Lester the less time I had to do the wrong things.

On one particular occasion before I won the national public speaking award, I was invited to speak at a WIRE conference in Florence, South Carolina. I didn't have transportation and needed a ride to get there. Being the guest speaker, I was told I could bring a parent if I chose to. My grandmother couldn't attend, and none of my aunts or uncles could take me, so I asked Mr. Lester if he could take me. He agreed to be my guest at the dinner. This would prove to be one of the proudest moments I would ever have with him. Mr. Lester was a simple, God-fearing man that remained the same no matter where or what the occasion. He had traveled before, but this event held particular significance for him.

Dad, Mr. Lester grew up before and during the civil rights movement. Discrimination and "whites only" and "coloreds not allowed" signs were commonplace to him but not to me. When we arrived at the function, we were among a room full of women, and none of them were African-American. It caused him to pause and reflect. It had become common place for me, but he had never been in a setting like this before. We were greeted graciously, and I introduced Mr. Lester as my best friend. They ushered him to one table and me to the head table at the podium where I would address the conference. During the meeting, dinner was served on a setting that was lovely. I could see him eating and looking around, and I wondered what he was thinking. When it was time for me to speak, I was introduced and the ladies applauded the mentioning of my accomplishments. A smile came across his face as he looked somewhat misty-eyed as if he might shed a tear. Mr. Lester beamed with pride as I gave my speech. It was a great feeling to look into an audience and see a familiar face. Mr. Lester was the first person to ever see me perform at a public speaking engagement. Until that moment no one had ever attended any of my speaking events. At the end of the meeting, everyone was so gracious and thanked us both for coming. They presented me with a check for $150.00, big money back then. Mr. Lester, sitting in his seat in amazement, began to stand, "Anthony, I'm so proud of you, Son."

I had never heard those words "I'm proud of you son" after a speaking engagement or competition, because I had always been there alone.

Mr. Lester remarked later, "This has been the first time in my life I ever sat in a room to eat and everyone was white." To me, that seemed foreign considering the places I had been and things I had seen. For him, it was quite to the contrary. He was used to having to sit at a different table or in a different room because of the color of his skin. In some cases, he remembered, "I didn't get to go in at all. You're too young to understand, but thank you for inviting me to come with you." Then jokingly he said, "You just got paid more than our pastor Rev. Backus for preaching on Sunday. Don't you mess up. You've come a long way, and I'm glad to have come with you." On the entire drive home, he talked about the experience. As a matter of fact, with everyone he talked to he had to share the feeling of being in that moment. I made history for him. It will always be important to remember the sacrifices of so many others who patiently waited and endured for the rest of us to have the freedoms we enjoy today.

The critique he gave me at my Head start play, when he told me to always hold my head up, and those countless talks and life lessons he shared with me had come full circle. I had given him a gift, and I had no idea it would mean so much to him. This was a remarkable man, and the single most influential man in my life. Why? He always found time to listen to me and always pointed out my flaws to fix so that I would become a better person. He never told me No without an explanation of why and then showed me a better way to do it. He never said Yes without extensive thought of the consequences that his answer would have. He never took his influence for granted and was well aware of his influence on my life. I have seen very few men today that have that character trait or are willing to share such wisdom. He took on your role, Dad, and he filled the void you left in my life. I only hope that in my lifetime to be a beacon of hope in the life of someone that shares the same *invisible pain*. As I continue to get older and deal with the pain of your absence, I often ask myself: what's your legacy as a father? Did you have a positive impact on anyone's life? Perhaps, you have, and one day I will have the opportunity to see for myself. I can only say that today, unfortunately, I only see you as a sperm donor. You threw your seed to the wind, and didn't take time to tend to the crop. You didn't care if the weeds and the tares destroyed it. You didn't water to see me grow, and protect me from harm. No, Dad, you just pretended the harvest was for others to protect and you lived your life without regard to the life you help create.

Your Son,

Anthony

DAD, EVERY TIME IT LOOKED IMPOSSIBLE, GOD STILL SHOWED ME FAVOR.

AT ONE TIME, I WORKED PART-TIME at a grocery store. The Jones family owned the local IGA store and taught me important life skills. They showed me how to stand out instead of blending in. They were extremely fair people and taught me how to interact with many different kinds of people, and often I had the opportunity to meet many of the local influential people in town. Known to be the cleanest grocery store and sell the best meats, IGA was not your typical privately-owned store. This family business offered great service and people shopped there for those reasons. There was a strict uniform for baggers, and I had to wear pressed white shirts and ties with jeans. Being clean cut, neat, and courteous was a major requirement, a reflection of the strong character and morals of the Jones family work ethic.

Ms. Jones introduced me to many people, one of whom was the assistant of a powerful senator of the state, Senator Saleeby. This would prove to be one of the biggest breaks of my life. The Jones' always encouraged me and never tried to hold me back or any of their employees who wanted to do better for themselves. She didn't have to do what she did, but it's a testament to the kindness of good people. That even the simplest jobs, if done well, can lead you to unimaginable opportunities.

Because of her kind gesture, Senator Saleebys' assistant and I began to talk often. I was always eager to bag his order of groceries when he came to the store. One day, I asked him if he would be kind enough to introduce me to the Senator. A bold request, but I was taught: You have not, because you ask not. "Let me see what I can do." Coincidentally about a month later, my uncle Bo had a meeting at the Saleeby law firm with an attorney involving a personal injury claim. Ms. Connie, a longtime receptionist for the firm, recognized me from the newspaper. We began to talk about my plans when she offered me congratulations. During our conversation, Senator Saleebys' assistant returned to the office. Ms. Connie, unaware we had been introduced at the grocery store, began to introduce us again. Once she realized we had met, she said, "Why don't you ask the Senator to make this young man a page in the senate? He's won national speaking awards." He answered he actually had been looking for the right time to introduce us. He invited me back to see if the Senator was available, and amazingly the Senator invited us into his office.

I was introduced as he rose from his big blue executive chair with the gold seal of South Carolina to shake my hand. I could tell he hadn't worked very hard. His hands were softer than the normal hands I was used to shaking. The assistant suggested I would be a great candidate to page and shadow him in the general assembly. There was no reply to this suggestion. He just wished me well and thanked me for coming in, and I was dismissed. In South Carolina, only a select few college students could become pages and it's quite an honor to be considered and an exceptional honor to be appointed. Thrilled and excited just to meet the Senator, I went back to the lobby to wait for my uncle to finish his appointment, eager to tell him where I had just been. I talked about that meeting the whole way home, and my grandmother was pleased as well.

Months later in late April, nearing the end of the school year, there was a letter on the kitchen table addressed to me from the Office of the Senate for State of South Carolina from Senator Saleeby. I quickly opened it to discover I was appointed to serve as a page in the general assembly. I had no idea he was even considering me since he didn't respond when the suggestion was made in his office. I didn't fill out an application or sit for an interview. God was truly looking out for me, even when I wasn't looking out for myself.

From the determination at 13 to work in the peach fields and from the kind gestures of the Jones family at the local grocery store, I was blessed with an appointment to page in the South Carolina Senate. Though you didn't teach me the value of work, I am grateful to those that stood in the gap for you, Dad. I was taught from an early age that there is honor in fair, legal work regardless of what the job entails. I was taught to never frown or be embarrassed at where you are today, for it's tomorrow that you will find hope to be in a better place and thankful for yesterday.

After years of fighting against myself, I was at a major turning point. It looked as if in spite of all I had done, I still didn't do enough. I was a nationally recognized public speaker and was fortunate enough to have been appointed to page for the Senate of South Carolina. Nevertheless, I was still failing, personally and academically. I was scrambling to graduate once again and had run into a brick wall.

I tried to fix the problem myself. I'm sure if I had informed my family what I was going through at the school, the situation would have ended in a different result. As usual, I was determined to do everything myself. Specifically, I was failing history in Ms. Tall's class. I missed taking a quiz while on an approved speaking engagement, and she gave me a "zero". Though I was given an approval by the principal, she refused to allow me to make up the quiz. Failing her class meant I wouldn't graduate. In her class, my final grade was a 69, and I needed a 70 to pass. Granted I hadn't put forth much effort in her class the whole year, but I still viewed her motives as hostile, unfair, and downright disgraceful at the time. It was the end of the school year, and there was no time to recover. I definitely was not going to come back next year to take one class, and more importantly, I would lose my page appointment. There was the option of summer school, but I wanted to march in the graduation ceremony. After all I had put my grandmother through, I wanted to prove her years of sacrifice weren't in vain.

Ms. Boltz' class was next door to Ms. Tall's, and I asked her to please talk to Ms. Tall and see if she could get her to change her mind. "Anthony, I can't make her change her mind, and I'm afraid I may not be able to help you with this one." However, true to her word and unwavering support, she tried. We stood in the hall at the end of the school day, and I pled my case as did Ms. Boltz. I remember saying, "Ms. Tall, I know I haven't been the best student, but I have represented this school well in all I have done. I am a nationally recognized public speaker and champion. I have been selected to serve as a page in the Senate. I'm regarded with high esteem across the state for winning every competition I've entered. Can you please allow me to take the missed quiz? Am I not worth at least one point so I can get my diploma and move on? Just round up my grade or let me take the quiz." I knew I could get a few points from a make-up quiz to push my average over the line. She looked at me with a stern cold look on her face and said, "No! No, you're not worth the one point. You've failed my class. There's nothing left to talk about." I will never forget that. I was so angry and wanted to retaliate in some way, and I felt that was what she wanted. She wasn't worth it. At the end of the day, I failed not only because I wasn't allowed to take the quiz nor wasn't given the needed point to pass, but I failed because of the countless times I refused to put forth the effort to do what was expected of me and what I was capable of doing. This remains a tough lesson to reflect on and was certainly a hard reality to live through. It was that painful and hostile moment that has made me more determined to never give that much power to anyone else again. I later realized that sometimes a hostile No ends up being a Yes when you are shown favor from God.

I looked for help elsewhere. I asked Senator Saleeby to see if he could or would help me. This was a big risk on my part, because I had to take my terrible transcripts and grades with me to show him. This was a man who thought I was a smart kid and was going to have to show him how much I had not applied myself in school. Everything was on the line – graduation and my page appointment. In my hand was a record of how much I had goofed off in the years past. As I walked into the office, I began to explain my problem to Ms. Connie. She immediately walked me back to the Senators' office. What's even more amazing is that he took the time from his busy schedule to listen to me. Dad, this was another wonderful man that I will be grateful to for his kind generosity as long as I live. He had me take a seat, and I told him my situation and gave him my poor transcripts. After listening without a word of intervention, he reached for his phone and immediately began to make calls on my behalf. It was my first time seeing how power, the right connections, and influence control everything. Sitting there witnessing how he handled himself, and the reactions of others to his requests, I was hooked and determined to surround myself with people who could move the ball forward rather than simply talking about it. I wanted some of this. I had never seen anything like that before.

He didn't bother to call my school; he went much higher than that. As he shared the situation with someone on the phone, the person happened to know about my public speaking awards and was amazed to hear the stand the school was taking on my imminent non-graduation. After a few calls, he told me to go home, not to worry about anything, to go back to school, and say nothing to anyone about our meeting. "Keep your nose clean, and don't get into any trouble. I'm going to make sure you graduate. Come back tomorrow after school, and I'll let you know where we stand." I went home to tell my grandmother what happened. Once again, she was very upset and quite disappointed we were back to my failing school again. I assured her everything was going to be all right. I had total confidence in Senator Saleeby.

Returning back to school the next day, I said nothing, not even to Ms. Boltz. I did exactly as I was instructed. After school, I returned to Senator Saleeby's office hoping for good news. I walked in and he said, "Look, I'm sorry you're not going to march or have a high school diploma from McBee High. There's not enough time to fight this." My heart sank. I really wanted to march and most of all leave high school. He then went on to say, "That does not mean we have lost the fight. What I can assure you is that you will have an official high school diploma, which is what's most important. You are a graduate in the eyes of the State of South Carolina. That's what matters. Although marching is symbolic, the diploma is reality." He gave me clear instructions on what I needed to do and sent me on my way. "This was just a minor problem, and always remember there's no problem in life that can't be solved by determination. I will see you in Columbia in the General Assembly as my page." Just like that. My problem was solved.

With the favor of God, I received my diploma and my fresh start. With the power of a praying Grandmother, a teacher who never gave up on me, an old family friend and mentor, and a state senator, I became the first man raised by my grandmother to graduate from high school. Although I didn't march at McBee, my high school years were finally behind me. Although I know there are always going to be obstacles in life, I refuse to give up.

I've learned to keep the faith and know that God always has a ram in the bush. Often it's the obstacles that save you from yourself as the miracles of God always strengthen and prepare you for blessings predestined as yours.

Sincerely

Anthony

DAD, I LEARNED A LESSON ABOUT PARENTING FROM SOMEONE I DIDN'T EVEN KNOW.

FINALLY, I WAS WORKING AS A page in the Senate and going to Benedict College in Columbia, South Carolina. Things were much different living on my own and there was excitement in being in the acquaintance of people I never imagined. As a page, to be in the same room as the governor, senators, and countless other powerful politicians was a major ego boost for a small town kid from the peach farms. I was in the midst of political giants. Living in the political bubble was all I wanted to do. Unfortunately, it was that exact mindset that got me into trouble in high school. I was spending too many hours at work with Senators, when I should have been in class at the college. I had become addicted being around powerful people. Unfortunately, there was no Ms. Boltz, no Mr. Lester, and no Grandmother in college to keep me out of trouble. As a page, I had a new furnished condo where other pages' and college students were living, a BMW to drive at will, and my life seemed as if it couldn't be any better. I became driven by money and the *presumption* of having the power which I didn't really have. I thought I had it all now. Look at me.

Instead of me seeing the page appointment as a stepping stone to greatness, I perceived it as final destination, because I never had anything. I had no direction, no identity, and still felt a sense of emptiness. I just went to college for the scholarship money, to follow a girl I liked, and to keep the page appointment. I didn't know the value of a college education. I didn't understand that. I saw the illusion instead. All I thought I had to do was hang out with these powerful people, and I would be just fine. Years of pretending and the lack of your guidance would prove I was not prepared for the real world, Dad.

My pretend games were now on steroids. The more I accomplished, the bigger I made it seem. I diminished my own smaller accomplishments by my need to look bigger and better than everyone else. I needed to prove to you, my absent father, that I had made it without you when in reality I hadn't. To me, it was never enough, and I kept setting goals that I couldn't achieve. I would tell myself I was doing better than I actually was. I was pretending to live a champagne life on a beer budget. I wasn't dealing with the small town crowd anymore; this was the big league. They didn't have to pretend to be from the right family or to have money like I would pretend to do. They actually had it. I was spending money like it was growing on trees although I had other obligations. I was in reality close to a complete meltdown. I wanted to do better and be better but had no idea how to do it.

I had no idea what a real father was or what it meant to have one, Dad. There was no real sense of understanding the responsibilities that fatherhood entailed. I didn't know you, so in my mind, I felt it meant nothing. I think now a stable two-parent home is a major plus, but that alone won't guarantee anything. The one thing it does is give you a fighting chance. Although I was living in a two-parent household, they were my grandparents. My mother would visit a few times a year, and I would visit her few times a year, but that's all I knew. I had been told lies from the beginning about you, so I too developed a pattern of lying. I basically called my grandmother and my mother both "Mom" and my granddad by Dad. I even called my step-father "Dad", as if he were truly my real dad, knowing very well he was not.

There were decisions to withhold information about you by everyone that have lasting effects and consequences on me. Looking back at this today, I have to ask: For what? Even you should be ashamed of yourself for the role you played in this cover-up. Silence does not give you an exemption from your guilt. When you keep secrets from your children, they begin to keep secrets from you. When adults lie and cover up family secrets, children develop a pattern of lying to cover internal secrets of their own.

I'm writing to you so I can understand who I am and who I was. Inside I didn't know who I was so I began to search for you so that if I knew you were, it would give me a better understanding of who I was. I had to be open and honest with myself - what I've done and why I did what I did. It's hard to value the truth if you don't know the truth. It is impossible to be honest with others when those you have trusted have not been honest with you. At some point, you get over that, put the past in front of you, deal with it, and then you can move on and put it behind you. Too often people want to put the past in the past without reflection or closure, but that never works. I have to forgive you, even if there is no hope in finding the truth.

It was a chance encounter with my friend Jim and his father that showed me a different glimpse of fatherhood. This was my first opportunity to see a father step up and solve a son's problem, without the son having to ask or depend on another man other than his father. Jim, also a page in the Senate, became one of my best friends. Jim often spoke of his father with high regards and respect although I did not meet him but once. Jim and I both had cars, and both of them broke down at the same time. Neither Jim nor I had the money to get our cars fixed, and I knew there was not $600.00 anywhere in my family for my car's repairs. Jim, however, called his father, told him of his situation, and early that Saturday morning there was a knock at the door. It was Jim's dad. After they left to go check on his car, I sat around wondering why I couldn't have had a father to show up for me and my almost identical situation.

By mid – afternoon, Jim and his dad returned, and Jim was very excited, because his father had bought him a new car. I was happy for Jim, but also jealous, because he had what I always wanted – not the car but the caring of a father. "Now, Jim, I gave you a new car, because you have given me happiness by being in school and doing well. Remember that when you have children. Always do the same for them that I have done for you. Stay in a position to help if the call comes. Remember, it's not about the car. It's about a father supporting his son." He hugged his son, and I never saw Jim's dad again. I also had never seen Jim cry until that morning. It wasn't for joy of having a new car, but because of the great love and bond he shared with his father. I had never seen anything like that before, and I remember almost wanting to cry myself. I knew at that moment I wanted to make sure my children would experience that feeling of a father being there, regardless of the sacrifices I might have to make for it to happen.

I was blessed to witness the responsibility of fatherhood before my eyes. It takes hard work, sacrifice, and dedication to define yourself as a real man. On that day, I learned the definition of a father. I vowed that my children would never go through life wanting and wondering what a supportive father looks like. Does this mean I am over a lot of hurt, pain, and resentment? No. However, I am better off than I was at the beginning of the journey. I realize I gave power to you, Dad, and made myself weak.

In this life, we are all given choices. There will be many decisions made that will have painful consequences. While I watched Jim have this relationship with his father, I wished for it with you. I wanted that kind of loving father-son relationship. While I witnessed this, I had my own two-year old son that I didn't have a relationship with. It wasn't that I was ignoring him, I just didn't understand what that father-son relationship was supposed to be. I didn't have one, so I wasn't conscious of not having one with my own child. My energy went into thinking about you being absent in my life rather than realizing I was absent in my own son's early life.

So I say to you, Dad, I don't write this letter to hurt you but to release my pain of feeling abandoned by you. In the end, I can never allow the pain to win, and I must always love you, even if you have never loved me.

Anthony

DAD, I'M THANKFUL FOR HAVING A STRONG PRAYING GRANDMOTHER.

IN THE MIDST OF WHAT SHOULD have been the greatest days of my life, I was feeling lower than I ever felt. I had a cool job and was making an impressive salary for a college student. I was living in a great condo. I had access to fine automobiles and could go anywhere I wanted to go. I made really great connections, because as a page I knew impressive people. There were problems. I was out of control with spending money and had begun to write checks to keep up with the charade of being rich. I looked the part but looks alone were deceiving. I didn't understand the value money, because I had never been taught how to save or manage money. In fact, I was making more as a page than my grandparents had made working a full time on the peach farm. Every time I would get into trouble, I would just say I was sorry, mention where I worked and who I worked for, and that solved everything. I managed to fix most things, but it didn't fix me. In the end, like everything else, you still fall and fall hard.

Finally, I had gone too far. I wrote a check that my rear end couldn't cash. I had robbed Peter to pay Paul for so long that I was about to go down in flames. I needed to cover a $600 check for car services, and I didn't have it. I thought surely by the time the check was presented for payment I would have the money, but that would not be the case. The dealership called, demanding their money. If I couldn't fix this, then I knew I would lose the job as a page, everyone would know that I had lied, my grandmother would find out I didn't know what I was doing, and my pretend life would start to crumble and fall around me. I saw no way out since it was all going to fail.

Scared, I felt the only thing to do was to die. I felt I had nothing to live for, so I came up with a plan to commit suicide. The pain had become so heavy, that I had lost all hope. I sat alone in my room not knowing what to do. I decided to make a formula that I knew would kill me and placed it under the kitchen sink. About 10:00 that morning, after my roommate had left, I sat in my living room waiting for the right time. I closed the blinds to make the room dark and sat there getting ready to die. My grandmother had given me a *Bible* to take to school with me, and I pulled it out and began to read the *23nd Psalm*. I knew it well, because it had always been my grandmother's favorite scripture.

After reading, I went into the kitchen, reached under the sink, and pulled out the formula. I dialed my grandmother's number, but she didn't answer the phone. She always answered, and this day I needed and wanted to hear her voice before it was over. I walked back into the living room, sat down, and opened the top of the bottle. As I started to put it to my mouth, there was a loud knock at the door. *Who in the world is that?* At first, I wasn't going to answer. No one knew I was home, so I just sat quietly looking at the bottle. Then there was another knock, this time louder, and I could tell they weren't going away. I put the bottle back under the sink and went to the door. Standing at the door was my grandmother and my uncles, Will and Bo. *That's* why she didn't answer the phone. God was sending her to *save* my life. I guess you could say this was my halleluiah moment and, Lord, please at the same time. To this day, I have no idea how the dealership got my grandmother's phone number, but they did and had called her for payment letting her know I was in trouble.

She told me I had a few minutes to get dressed and ready. It was clear I was not going to be in charge. "I don't want to hear anything you have to say. Bring me that checkbook and let's go." We took a road trip to the dealership, and I was forced to meet face to face with the owner. I didn't want to do it, but she told me, "Today, you're going to be a man. You were man enough to do it, now you're going to be man enough to fix it." Grandma's firm look said, "God is now testing your character, Anthony. The question is: Can you pass the test? You may lose face, honor, and even credibility, but to be a man, you must always face your problems. By facing them, you will find victory and will always be greater than your problems." Through those words, I learned the only true test of character is your ability to rise above adversity and your pride.

I ate a lot of humble pie that day, but had she not shown up I surely would have killed myself for no good reason. I selfishly chose death instead of just talking and asking for help. When you can't do it on your own, there is always comfort in the word of God. I knew the power of prayer, even in the midst of doing the wrong thing. The grace of God saved me as I sat and read the *23nd Psalm*. If I hadn't sat there and reflected on that passage, praying my last prayer, my grandmother wouldn't have gotten there in time to save me.

I was hurting inside from the pain of feeling rejected and had convinced myself that the only way out was to die. Sometimes the love of others just isn't good enough, you have to love yourself first, and I had no idea how to do that. I hadn't learned to love myself, because I was always searching for acceptance from people that weren't interested in loving me the way I wanted to be loved. Searching and waiting for you, Dad, wasted so much time and energy that I failed to see the many blessings I had been given. I never learned how to be satisfied with who I was and became addicted to trying to be someone I was not.

My addiction wasn't overeating, drinking, or drugs. Mine was an addiction to pretend to be what I was not. Pretending to be something I wasn't to fill the void of an invisible father consumed me so much until I failed to be the best person I could be. When my grandmother and uncles left me at the condo later that day still unaware they had saved my life, I knew I had to make some changes or I was going to self-destruct. I went back into the kitchen and reached under the sink and pulled out the bottle and looked at it for what seemed like hours. I finally poured it down the drain, opened the blinds, and said to myself: *It's time to go but not time to die.*

The next morning, I went downtown to the military recruiter's office to enlist. Outside the Army recruiter station, I saw two Marines walking down the sidewalk. They were dressed in their dress blue uniforms, having just performed duties at as honor guards at a funeral. "Man, that's a nice uniform." I said. "You can have one, too." They answered. I changed from being almost Army to a Marine at that moment. I needed discipline and direction. Going back home was not an option. I wanted more. I had tasted the world of business and power, and I was determined I wasn't going back. I was determined to make it, but how I had been going about it was not going to work. In order for me to live and survive, I needed to leave college. I had been given a great opportunity, but at the same time, I was not ready for it. Being a page was quick success, but I had no foundation to be successful later or to know there was more beyond just begin a page in the moment. Instant gratification is often short lived, and if you're not prepared and ready mentally for what comes later, what looks like a blessing can easily become a curse.

First, I went to Senator Saleeby's office and told him I was leaving for the military, thanking him for everything he had done for me. He was disappointed but wished me well. Then I went back home to tell my grandmother my plans, and she didn't like them at all. "You're on your own now. All I can do is pray for your life, health, and strength. I'm sad for you to go, but I don't have anything to offer you to stay. If you're going to leave and you are going to just go work on a farm, then you can stay here. If you're going to leave and you are going to just go work in a grocery store, then you can stay here. If you're going to leave and go work in a plant, then you can stay here and work at the factory. But if you are going to go do something different and better yourself than what you've already done, then you go." When the time came, I left with nothing more than a prayer and a dream to one day make my grandmother proud. Ironically, my mother had left for New York with a similar dream when she reached her turning point in life. I wanted to give my grandmother more, even though she was satisfied with less. I was determined to rise above my adversities, and the *invisible pain* buried deep inside of me. Even then, I had no idea how deep my *pain* really was buried.

As I entered into the Marine Corp, I was now becoming a man under the guidance of rules that would shape my life and help me to grow up into a responsible contributor to society. Though the battles continue, I have yet to accept defeat. Opening the window of my life about the *internal pain* I have because of you is difficult but rewarding. Dad, I realize it's only the end if you accept defeat and surrender. If these words find you, and you are in a mind to understand the pain, then my prayer is that you ask God to forgive you. The love of Christ will always be the one thing that will last and stand the test of time. Remember, you don't have to look like what you're going through, and wherever you find yourself in life, there is always someone willing to change places with you. So, Dad, wherever you are in life, I pray that if I have brothers and sisters and that you have loved them unconditionally, been a better father for them than you have been for me.

Sincerely,

your Son anthony

DEAR READER,

EVERY DECISION WE MAKE IN LIFE has consequences. From the time you open our eyes in the morning until the time you close them at the end of your day, the choices you make not only affect you but everyone around you and in your life. Never lose yourself by allowing the choices of others to dictate your own choices. The pain inflicted on you, either *visible* or *invisible*, physical or emotional, will forever hold power over you unless you find the strength from within to forgive. Your healing must include a self-examination of your contributions to your pain as well as the contribution of others. Many times we find it easier to blame everyone else rather than accepting personal responsibility for our own suffering.

Though painful to accept and understand, your personal suffering does not give you the right to inflict agony on others. For years, I prayed for the wrong things. I wanted to inflict or witness pain on others that I felt had done me wrong rather than ask God for forgiveness for the thing I had done wrong. I've often found myself comfortable going months, if not years, without associating with people I felt hurt me for whatever reason. Justified or not, it hasn't been worth it and it's not the right thing to do. We often want to be forgiven for our sins toward others but feel it unnecessary to forgive for the things we have done. Victory does not belong to us; it only belongs to God. Through this process of self-examination, I have learned that many of my personal struggles have been of my own making. My advice to those that read these letters to my dad is simply this: *Deal with your pain before your pain deals with you.* Nothing can make up for what you've lost. You must accept it for what it is and release your pain to God. The agony of fighting a battle that you will never win on your own will bring nothing more than continued pain. Some things you have to let go and let God.

Though I yearned for a father in my mind as you can see, God provided many wonderful men to watch over me during those challenging years. Regardless of what you feel inside, know that you are never alone. Though life's trials and tribulations often feel impossible to bear, know that it's never over unless God says it's over. Being a father is reality; however, many men only see it as fiction. It's a calling, a charge ordained by God to provide, protect, and defend the life you created. It's equally important to note that many men can't be what they've never witnessed or never have been taught to be. We now live in a society of fatherless homes, and sometimes even if the father lives there. Fine homes, money, and expensive possessions will never serve as a substitute for love and support. Anyone that follows this path will certainly witness a recipe for disaster. Some think they have answered the call of being the ideal father, only to realize the call has not been answered. By no means do I say I have answered the call in every way. It took years to come to the reality that I had no idea what I was doing. Even now, I make mistakes. My only desire is that you, the reader, will take a moment to be aware and save another son or daughter from years of *invisible pain.*

If you, Reader, are the one without a parent, finding internal healing will yield a better result than external excuses. We are who we are, and we have been given the power and the choice to rise above our faults, our *pain*, and our circumstances. Find a way to use your pain to empower others. I do feel that my pain is like the pain of many others. Together we can rise above the pain and not allow it to defeat us or hold us hostage from the destiny to live a fulfilled life.

Although I didn't have a father in my life, I was blessed with so many people who were positive influences. Mr. Lester guided me and watched over me. Mrs. Boltz was challenging and never gave up on me. The Jones family introduced me to Senator Saleeby's circle. And my grandmother, who through it all when everyone else had given up on me, never gave up and told me, "You can rise above any failure. Never accept defeat. Always find a way to do the impossible." When others don't believe in you, you have to believe in yourself.

If you've never met your father or mother or perhaps you know them and feel empty because of their inability to connect to you, I ask you to follow the path as I have. Write a letter to them. Know that through the love of God you have the power to heal from the wounds of *Invisible Pain*.

All the Best,

Anthony

THE TRUTH AND THE LIE

It starts as a small mustard seed, planted and fertilized.
To live and to grow,
It requires more attention than many may ever realize.

Now there is a beautiful garden of greens for the entire world to see,
There's more to the creation of life than giving birth to me.

I lost myself in search of you, though you never knew.
I was left to search on my own, not really knowing what to do.
For me, it would've been so much easier if I had just learned the truth from you.

Now the weeds have suppressed the life of that forgotten seed that didn't really grow.
It's left without a true identity. What will happen, for some, we may never know?

Like seeds in a garden left untilled, from the infested weeds of the earth,
You've lost the identity of your seed you carried for nine months until birth.

When secrets shelter the truth from shining, the lie lives on forever.
When I think of the story of my life, the truth would've been so much better.

A lie take's on a new identity each and every time it's told,
By the time you reach the truth, a different story begins to unfold.

The flesh will live, but one day must surely die,
For this, we have no control. There must be truth to the flesh, or the legacy remains a lie.

www.ingramcontent.com/pod-product-compliance
Lightning Source LLC
Chambersburg PA
CBHW070636030426
42337CB00020B/4034